D0502552

The Day After the Dollar Crashes

The Day After the Dollar Crashes

A Survival Guide for the Rise of the New World Order

Damon Vickers

WILEY

John Wiley & Sons, Inc.

Copyright © 2011 by Damon Vickers. All rights reserved.

Published by John Wiley & Sons, Inc., Hoboken, New Jersey.
Published simultaneously in Canada.

No part of this publication may be reproduced, stored in a retrieval system, or transmitted
in any form or by any means, electronic, mechanical, photocopying, recording, scanning,
or otherwise, except as permitted under Section 107 or 108 of the 1976 United States
Copyright Act, without either the prior written permission of the Publisher, or
authorization through payment of the appropriate per-copy fee to the Copyright
Clearance Center, Inc., 222 Rosewood Drive, Danvers, MA 01923, (978) 750-8400, fax
(978) 646-8600, or on the Web at www.copyright.com. Requests to the Publisher for
permission should be addressed to the Permissions Department, John Wiley & Sons, Inc.,
111 River Street, Hoboken, NJ 07030, (201) 748-6011, fax (201) 748-6008, or online at
http://www.wiley.com/go/permissions.

Limit of Liability/Disclaimer of Warranty: While the publisher and author have used
their best efforts in preparing this book, they make no representations or warranties
with respect to the accuracy or completeness of the contents of this book and specifically
disclaim any implied warranties of merchantability or fitness for a particular purpose. No
warranty may be created or extended by sales representatives or written sales materials.
The advice and strategies contained herein may not be suitable for your situation. You
should consult with a professional where appropriate. Neither the publisher nor author
shall be liable for any loss of profit or any other commercial damages, including but not
limited to special, incidental, consequential, or other damages.

For general information on our other products and services or for technical support, please
contact our Customer Care Department within the United States at (800) 762-2974,
outside the United States at (317) 572-3993 or fax (317) 572-4002.

Wiley also publishes its books in a variety of electronic formats. Some content that appears
in print may not be available in electronic books. For more information about Wiley
products, visit our web site at www.wiley.com.

ISBN 978-0-470-91033-7 (cloth); 978-1-118-02354-9 (ebk);
978-1-118-02358-7 (ebk); 978-1-118-02355-6 (ebk)

Printed in the United States of America
10 9 8 7 6 5 4 3 2

To all the children in the world who will inherit
the results of a million choices made before them
and who, with love, may yet get the chance
to create a new world for themselves.

Contents

Acknowledgments

I want to acknowledge my wife, Luiza, for all her support over the years and giving me three beautiful daughters who mean the world to me.

I especially want to thank my editor, researcher, and collaborator Leslie vanWinkle, for pulling this book together from all my ideas and keeping me on track. This book would not exist without her. Thanks also go out to staff member Caroline Fernandes for her help with our research.

Introduction

Thank you for picking up this book. It means a lot to me to get this message out to people. I hope you will be moved to talk to your friends and communities about the ideas you find here.

We are at a crossroads. Our global economic stability is in jeopardy; our planet's ecosystems are under attack, physical health is not valued; and the westernized lifestyle is totally unsustainable. And we have run out of time.

Huge changes are coming whether or not we want or are ready for them. My gift to you is a book full of information that can help you prepare for, adapt to, and flourish during and after this transformation.

Here you'll find a possible time line for the crash of the U.S. dollar and the subsequent collapse of global markets. I outline the New World Order I foresee taking shape over the next decade and the impact it will have on how nations govern, how businesses conduct transactions, how resources are managed, and how we as individuals will care for ourselves and the planet.

In support of this inevitable evolution, I've identified industries, systems, and lifestyle choices that are unsustainable and destructive to the health of this planet and every living creature on it. I've included warnings about potential obstacles and resistance this evolution may face from people who are seriously invested in the status quo. And there will be resistance.

Yet I've also identified several budding social trends that, if supported by major changes in social behavior, could drive businesses to meet new demands and evolve into The Next Big Thing.

It won't be the first time I've spotted a winning trend. My track record is full of them. I've been an investor for over 25 years and come from a family with a long tradition of service in the financial industry. Between me, my father, my grandfather, and my great grandfather, my family has about 160 years cumulative experience in the stock market. I'm well-grounded in the core principles of managing risk and investing wisely.

Still, I believe that it is my very unconventional upbringing that has prepared me for the unique challenges we are all facing now. That is why I believe I'm the right person to write about what comes next.

I come from a family of great wealth, yet I spent many of my early years in poverty, and my teenage years at the Buddhist monastery, Odiyan. I understand the social responsibility of wealth, the pain of uncertainty, and the truth of our Oneness.

I have learned compassion for people damaged by life and have learned to respect those who courageously overcome their challenges. My spiritual training has given me mental discipline and objectivity, which allows me to see through misleading information the media feeds us, to see the underlying truth, and to trade what the market gives me.

I've had a rags-to-riches-to-rags-to-riches career, and the hardships of my youth have taught me to remain fluid and adaptable even when circumstances change. And the world is changing very rapidly now. My whole life seems to have been pointed toward teaching me to think for myself and to stand by my convictions even when they aren't popular or don't align with the conventional wisdom many people consider safe.

The truth is this: The economic situation in the world is not safe. We are at a crossroads and we need new ideas if we're going to thrive. My goal with this book is to help you fill that need.

The current economic climate and the accelerating destruction of our environment and our bodies make our coming decisions and choices critical. I can't state this strongly enough. Our economy and our environment are at risk. Our very lives and the lives of our children are at stake. The time for denial and waiting for someone else to fix everything is over. It is up to us, each and every one of us, to wake up and start to make more responsible choices as we usher in a New World Order.

And that, my friends, will be The Next Big Thing.

Chapter 1

We Are in Deep Trouble and We're Not Alone

We are at a crossroads of immense proportions. Nationally, internationally, and globally, we are living in a manner that is absolutely, unconditionally, irrevocably unsustainable.

The United States and our fellow nations are facing an Armageddon of economic collapse as every nation slowly spins into a death spiral, pulled down by debt that appears impossible to repay.

As a global economic community, we are scrabbling for any toehold on a slippery rock face, clinging by our broken, bleeding nails from the very edge of a precipice as we peer down into the abyss.

We may fall unless we get a grip.

Today's Reality

As a nation, the United States has enjoyed many decades of growth where our main economic function was to consume. Over the last

1

10 years in particular, all the chickens have come home to roost. The seeds we have sown with our indulgent living and our toxic relationship with our planet have created severe and blatant problems, not only for ourselves, but for the world.

As a nation the United States can no longer fool itself, and the rest of the world, into believing that everything is okay; because everything is very much not okay. Below is a summary of just some of the challenges facing the United States, all of which put downward pressure on the U.S. dollar.

- Right now the United States has a negative $65 trillion net worth and is seriously underwater.
- Right now the United States imports $800 billion in oil every year.
- Right now the disparity in wages between the United States and the rest of the world makes it impossible for the United States to compete globally, and we are losing jobs and our economic edge to emerging nations.
- Right now we are digging a hole to China with unfunded debt.
- Right now we spend $2.4 trillion a year on health care and no one is getting any healthier!
- Right now our government is obligated to pay increasing amounts of social security benefits and Medicare entitlements.
- Right now we are damaging our life support systems and poisoning future generations.
- Right now we plow under our farmland and are net importers of food. We were once the breadbasket of the world and now we don't even feed ourselves.
- The food we do produce is saturated with toxins and hormones that act as endocrine disrupters and have been strongly associated with increases in reproductive problems and cancers in many species, including humans.

I'll get into detail on these issues in a bit, but the bottom line is that all of these things combined are pushing the U.S. dollar to collapse.

With so many challenges it is easy to feel ineffectual and to fall into despair. But with these momentous changes come momentous opportunities. That is what we must focus on.

We Are Not a Going Concern

We have a plague of overleveraged debt that is unsustainable. Right now the United States has a negative $65 trillion net worth and is seriously underwater. If you think of each U.S. dollar as a share of common stock in a company, then we can think of the United States as functionally bankrupt while the Board of Directors and the government tell lies to the shareholders, who are the taxpayers, you.

As a country we are not a going concern. We don't fuel our cars. We don't keep ourselves healthy. We don't feed our bellies. We don't make anything anymore! We don't make real things, real goods, or real services and earn real capital. We don't export things. We are not producing sufficient income. Yet the government trots out statistics that try to tell a different story, so that the next bond auction gets completed.

It has long been a tradition for American economic leaders to look to the Gross Domestic Product (GDP) numbers as a way to measure the health of our country. Economic leaders look at the numbers every quarter and the President trots it out at every State of the Union address.

Supposedly, the GDP denotes the country's economic growth. We are told that if our GDP grew by such and such a number then we are okay. As long as the economy is growing then we can have confidence that our system is sound. We are told that growth will inevitably bail us out of our pesky debt problems. We are told that if the statistics say that America is strong, that Europe is strong, and that Italy is strong, then we have no need to worry.

This fable has been around so long people have actually stopped questioning it. But every journalist, statistician, and politician knows that these numbers are subject to constant revision and can be manipulated to tell any story. What everyone doesn't know is that these GDP numbers are already flawed.

The gross domestic product (GDP) measures output generated through property-related business like rentals and production by labor that is physically located within a country's borders. It excludes income earned by U.S. citizens working overseas and so does not reflect income generated by companies with overseas operations. However, it does reflect trade within our own borders and among our own businesses and counts those transactions as product sales. This is not a true picture of our domestic production.

Trade within our own borders is not a product at all. Any retailer will tell you that moving a package from one counter to another counter doesn't mean it left the store as a sale. We are focused at looking at the GDP number as if it denoted the economic health and viability of our country, when in truth that number tells a distorted story.

Our GDP numbers don't show real exports; they are the results of an internal shell game where U.S. refineries sell to U.S. manufacturers, who sell to U.S. consumers. It's all self-dealing; it isn't new money coming into the country. Even so, you can see by the chart in Figure 1.1 prepared by ShadowStats that the GDP has been steadily falling over the past few decades. What is interesting is that the top line reflects the official statistics, while the bottom line reflects the more accurate statistics, having incorporated factors ignored by the government.

The real economic viability of any country should be based on its ability to sell things, to trade with the rest of the world, and to earn capital. That is what we used to do. If we look at the United States during the 1800s and 1900s, we were a rip-roaring growing economy. The real traders and consumers in the world were the Europeans, and the United States benefited. After Europe devoured its own lumber then devoured all the hardwoods and mahogany in the Caribbean, the United States exported American lumber. Our forests were our GDP,

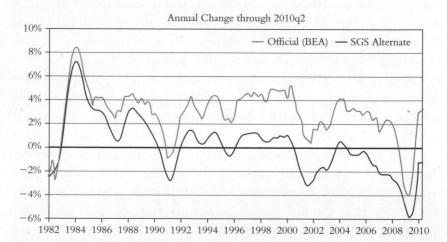

Figure 1.1 GDP Annual Growth—Official versus SGS
Source: Chart courtesy of ShadowStats.com. *Data Source:* SGS, BEA.

so we cut them all down and shipped them overseas and now we don't have them anymore. Already 97 percent of the U.S. forests have been cut down and the timber companies are lobbying to get to the last 3 percent!

Plus, we incur additional massive national debt by importing everything from construction machinery to Royal Bee Jelly, including oil. Right now the United States imports $800 billion worth of oil every year, which is money that leaves our borders.

The only real gauge of our worth is in what we export. Unfortunately, the main thing the United States exports is debt and its hollow promises in the form of derivatives and Treasury notes. And of the items we do export, we are seeing a growing imbalance as we import more than we export.

Our trade balance has steadily increased to the negative side for the past 20 years. To give you an idea of just how lopsided that ratio is, Table 1.1 is a summary of how a few of our manufacturing sectors are doing, according to the U.S. Foreign Trade Division of the U.S. Census Bureau.

We Are a Society Dependent on Entitlements

Part of our national debt can be laid at the door of our expectations. In addition to the $13 or $14 trillion the United States already owes, we've got another $60 to 80 trillion in unfunded liabilities for existing social entitlements and another $40 to $50 trillion in promises for new entitlements.

And the United States doesn't have the money to pay for these entitlements. It doesn't exist. We are already in debt. According to the ShadowStats statistics, we are currently experiencing between 16 and 20 percent unemployment, contrary to the 9 percent in the government's official reports. This means 20 percent of our population is not working and not paying payroll taxes into the Treasury. That translates to a diminishing tax base that will continue to diminish unless we get those people back to work or the government raises taxes. Which means the money won't be there to fund all these entitlements. Nor is it likely that we'll be able to convince other countries to buy any more of our Treasuries to fund these obligations.

Table 1.1   Examples of Exports for Selected Manufacturing Sectors

Imports	Exports	20-Year Change in U.S. Export/Import
Computer and Electronic Product Manufacturing		
The total imports in this sector in 2009 were about 4 times the 1989 total. Imports from China increased almost 90 times during those 20 years, from less than 2% to almost 40%. Imports also increased from Mexico (7 times) and Malaysia (5 times), while imports from Japan dropped about 40%.	Exports to China increased about 14 times, to Canada by about 3.5 times, and Mexico by about 3 times, while exports to the United Kingdom and Germany remained about the same.	−$105,984,506,807
Electrical Equipment, Appliance, and Component Manufacturing		
This is a similar story. Imports from China increased about 30 times over those 20 years while Japanese imports fell 21%.	Exports to China increased about 14 times, to Canada by about 3.5 times, and to Mexico by about 3 times, while exports to the United Kingdom and Germany remained about the same.	−$24,642,288,144
Transportation Equipment Manufacturing		
Other than Canada and Japan, Mexico became one of the biggest players in the imports of transportation equipment, an increase to 20% share of the total imports from 5% 20 years ago. In the same period, Canada and Japan lost the shares of 10% and 15%, respectively.	Again China took the lead, increasing its demand for U.S. goods by about 10 times since 1989. Mexico's demand increased by 4 times, Canada's increased by about 30%, and again, exports to the United Kingdom and Germany remained about the same.	−$14,837,319,678

This is a critical situation. In the face of this math and in the face of a quickly increasing population of aging and retiring Baby Boomers, we can see that something has to give. It is very likely many of those with expectations of entitlements will not see them. Or if they do, they will be reduced and payable in deflated U.S. dollars.

In 2009, the U.S. government paid Social Security benefits to 7.7 million people for a total of $46 billion. This included nonretirees with medical or mental problems or disabilities. Of this figure, over half of the recipients relied on their Social Security payments as their only reported income.

According to the 2004 Trustees to the Social Security Administration, 2009 began the decline in the amount of money coming into the funds and by 2018 the cost of the program will exceed the income tax. They went on to say that at that point the accumulated trust fund assets of about $2.3 trillion (in 2004 dollars) will start to be used to augment the tax income so that scheduled benefits can continue to be paid in full.

Table 1.2 will give you an idea of how well funded the Social Security benefits program is and how soon it is projected to be depleted. These estimates track the four main trust funds and are based on 2003 projections conducted by the U.S. Social Security Administration Division of Economic Research.

Supposedly, the money we take out of the Social Security fund is money that we paid into the system, or that people before us paid into the system. Many people feel we've earned this money and that may or may not be true. If we've worked hard and paid our taxes then perhaps we do deserve a bit of help when we're no longer able to do those things, but as a society we have come to believe that we deserve these things regardless of how hard we've worked or not worked.

The generation currently in power in the United States has never had to consider a future that didn't have these safety nets. Thus, we have not developed a proper respect for these things, nor appreciation of them. We have never given serious thought about how we would survive our golden years without them. As a result, most of us have not made other arrangements, and that is not good because the current system is not prepared to handle the coming demand as the Boomers retire and our population becomes frailer.

Table 1.2   Projected Trust Fund Exhaustion Dates under Assumptions of the 2002 Trustees' Report

Model	Low Range	Intermediate Range	High Range
Stochastic models			
CBOLT	2028	2037	2063
TL	2029	2037	2056
SSASIM	a	2037/2038	a
OCACT	2034	2041	2057
Standard model (Trustees' Report)	2029	2041	b

Note: For the stochastic models, the low-, intermediate-, and high-range results are for the 10th, 50th, and 80th percentile, respectively. For the Trustees' Report, the three ranges are for the low-cost, intermediate, and high-cost assumptions in the 2002 Trustees' Report.
[a] SSASM modeled only two variables—productivity and fertility—stochastically, so the range of outcomes should not be compared with those of the other stochastic models.
[b] According to the low-cost projections in the 2002 Trustees' Report, the trust funds are not exhausted at the end of the 75-year projection period.

This is already an unsustainable situation, yet now we've heaped another huge obligation on top of those in the form of our new Obama Care program. This is a nightmare that we can't wake up from. Already health care in this country is a staggering expense. The programs scheduled to start in 2014 will cripple us unless we take some drastic action.

Our Aging Population Is Expensive

The elephant in the living room is getting bigger. We have a huge bulge of Baby Boomers getting older and they are already taking a toll on the U.S. Treasury with their Social Security claims and Medicare claims. We can expect this population to require more and more health care as they grow older. To understand just how draining these needs will be, you need to understand the dynamics of this population.

The older population (65 years of age and older) increased 15 percent from 35 million in 2000 to 40 million in 2010 and is expected to increase another 36 percent over the next decade to 55 million in 2020 (see Figure 1.2 and Table 1.3).

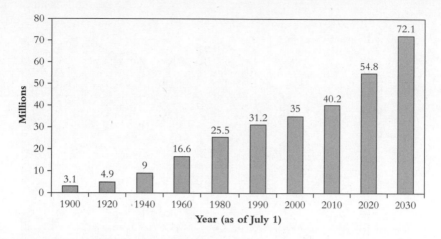

Figure 1.2   Number of Persons 65+ by 2030
Source: U.S. Census Bureau, Population Division.

What's more, we are seeing people live much longer than in the past. The 85 years of age and older population has increased 36 percent since 2000 and is projected to increase another 15 percent in the next decade from 5.7 million in 2010 to 6.6 million in 2020.

According to census data, as of 2009, people age 65+ totaled about 33 percent of the U.S. population. This is already a huge number.

In the U.S. Census chart shown in Figure 1.3, you can see the growth of this demographic. Think of all the costs associated with aging and it is clear that we have hostaged our future and the future of our children to pay for a Social Security system and a Medicare system that are already gargantuan Ponzie schemes that make Bernie Madoff's trick look like a carousel ride.

Table 1.3   Number of Persons 60+

Age Group	1990	2000	2000–2009
60 & Over	11.9%	12.8%	18.0%
65 & Over	8.0%	8.5%	12.9%
85 & Over	1.5%	1.2%	1.8%

SOURCE: U.S. Census Bureau, Population Division.

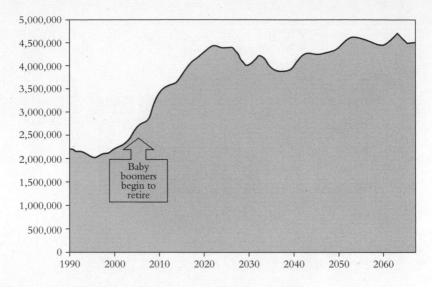

Figure 1.3 The Baby Boomers Began Retiring in 2008
Note: The number of Baby Boomers retiring each year will increase 60 percent over the next 20 years.
Source: U.S. Census Bureau.

I'm not political, but I am analytical. When we add the anticipated costs associated with the Obama health care program to this already heavily over-leveraged system, it is clear that we have created a monster that will devour several generations to come, provided it can even survive.

The United States is not the only country with this problem. The demographic impacts on France, Greece, Spain, Portugal, Italy, and several other European countries, as well as Canada, are just as immense. Like the United States, these are mature economies with aging populations. Like the United States, they will struggle to meet the demands of an aging population.

According to the Department of Economic and Social Affairs, the number of people worldwide over the age of 60 has tripled over the last 50 years and will more than triple again by 2050 (see Figure 1.4). By then, 33 countries are projected to have more than 10 million people over 60. China, India, The United States, Brazil, and Indonesia are projected to have more than 50 million people in that group.

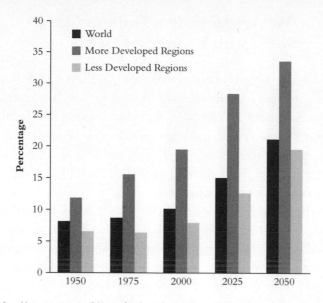

Figure 1.4 Proportion of Population Age 60 or Over (World and Developing Regions, 1950–2050)
Source: Department of Economic and Social Affairs.

These mature economies are confronted with the need to provide for the social needs of their growing populations. Those social needs include food, shelter, medical care, and in many cases jobs as retirees find they still need to generate income. These populations have been led to expect a certain standard of living and quality of life and they believe they are entitled to them. We can expect more upheaval as people realize these entitlements are not arriving on schedule, or they are told that the retirement age is being moved to 70.

As the pressure to meet these expectations increases, countries will find their options lessening. Options include going to war to get more resources from other countries, reducing those expectations by cutting benefits, or adopting a one-child policy to deal with the reality of too many people and not enough food and jobs to go around. The first option would be disastrous, the second option is probably likely, and the third is too little too late since a one-child policy will simply reduce the size of the working population and further skew the ratio between the number of people paying into the treasuries and the number of people draining the treasuries.

We Are Digging a Hole to China
with Unfunded Debt

The world is choking on debt. Every month the United States has to raise money to pay for our lifestyle by selling bonds at auctions. The problem is that there isn't enough demand for our bonds on a global basis. When China and other countries balked at recent bond auctions, the Fed simply printed more money and the U.S. government bought its own debt. When this happens, we tell the world that the debt auctions were oversubscribed two-to-one.

It's a whopping lie! Everyone knows it's a lie and it makes us look incompetent. Printing money is the Fed's solution to the problem of other countries' lost confidence in the value of our securities. We print our own money to buy our own paper because no one else wants in the game. This kind of self-dealing is absolutely unsustainable and positively incestuous.

How much money are we talking about? It is difficult to get accurate numbers on how much money the Fed has printed. The government tracks the money supply using a measurement called M3. The ups and downs of this M3 measurement are a pretty good gauge of how much money is pouring into the economy. But the Fed has been printing money and adjusting interest rates to manipulate the money supply for so long that these tools don't work very well anymore. In fact, in March of 2006 the Federal Reserve stopped reporting the M3 entirely. I don't think they even know how much money is in the system anymore.

But the Fed's practice of printing money and controlling interest rates is not new. According to The Money Masters (www.themoney masters.com), the Federal Reserve stopped the 1993 recession by printing money at an annual rate of 13 percent. The flood of money helped fuel the stock market frenzy in the late 1990's. Then as the market was hitting the ceiling in 2000, the Fed hit the brakes and we saw the market bubble collapse two years later (see Figure 1.5).

A potential financial meltdown spooked the Fed, so they started printing money again. This money was so available and cheap the low interest rates encouraged a massive increase in consumer spending

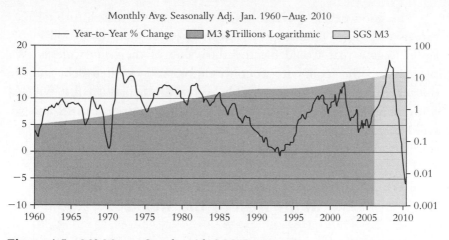

Figure 1.5   M3 Money Supply with SGS Continuation

The 2010 downward slope reflects year-over-year statistics through the 2nd quarter of 2010; it doesn't necessarily mean the money supply is shrinking as a whole.

Source: ShadowStats.com. SGS extended data provided through other sources in the absence of official Federal Reserve statistics.

and home loans. This fueled a strong stock market and the real estate bubble that started in 2002 and ended with a thud in 2007, overleveraging everyone and resulting in the meltdown in 2008.

Between 2005 and 2008, the U.S. money supply increased from $10 trillion to $14 trillion dollars. That is a whopping 40 percent increase. Now if you just use the rate of increase in the money supply chasing as an indicator of inflation, the actual rate of inflation between 2005 and 2008 is nearly 13 percent per year.

As of 2010, the Fed is still printing money, although not as much as during their peak press operations in 2008. They are trying to fight deflation, which adds to my belief that the U.S. dollar will continue to decline and force a restructuring of our currency.

So our money is cheap, our interest rates low, and the reality is that we are hostage to foreign nations who own our bank. The United States no longer controls its own money. China. Saudi Arabia. India. They buy our bonds. They buy our bundled mortgages and the hundreds of derivatives that are still floating around out there. They own the future of our children.

The good news I have to offer in the face of this disturbing picture is that other countries do not want to see the U.S. dollar collapse because that would destroy the value of their investments. We can expect other countries to continue to prop up their debt and the dollar's value, which could possibly soften the fall. But fall it will. At some point some unseen hand will shake this house of cards and we will likely have some predictable outcomes.

We Export Our Consumer-Oriented Lifestyle to the Rest of the World

As a nation, the United States has enjoyed nearly 50 years of growth where our main economic function has been to consume. Over the last decade in particular this obsession with acquiring material possessions and our indulgent living have created severe and blatant problems not only for us, but for the world.

The 1990s saw tremendous growth in the United States. Hundreds of companies went public: Starbucks, Cisco, and the whole tech boom. We had a bull market! That growth changed the world and when it began running out of steam in 2003, banks added fuel to the fire by encouraging people to borrow against their home equity to buy more stuff.

Our consumer-based society of the United States became the economic model for most of the Western world, and now Greece, Portugal, Spain, England, France, and dozens of other countries are dealing with unsustainable debt right along with us.

So, what can we do?

Well, we can't fix the problems of those other countries, but we can fix our own. Most people by now have figured out that depleting our personal assets for short-term indulgences leaves us in a very uncertain situation. If you haven't already tapped all your assets, don't. For your peace of mind alone, you need to have a buffer and it only makes sense to keep something back for potential financial drains. If you are already flat-out busted, start to build a buffer. It comes down to day-to-day choices about what you need versus what you want. We can't possibly expect our government to get their financial house in order if we as individuals can't do it first.

We Cannot Compete Globally Due to the Disparity in Wages

We are already seeing the results of the disparity in wages between the United States and other nations. Compared to the rest of the world, the wages paid in the United States are humongous. Grand Canyonesque.

Production labor in China, India, East Asia, Eastern Europe, or Mexico costs a fraction of what it costs in the United States.

As of 2008, the hourly cost of producing a product in China was 9.48 yuan per hour, which is the equivalent of $1.36 USD per hour (see Table 1.4).

As of 2005 the hourly cost of producing a product in India averaged 20.06 rupees, which was the equivalent of $0.91 USD per hour (see Table 1.5).

Data through 2008 indicates that what costs $30 per hour to produce in the United States costs around $15 per hour in East Asia, about $10 per hour in Eastern Europe, and around $5 per hour in Mexico (see Figures 1.6, 1.7, and 1.8).

As you can see from the charts, the United States simply cannot compete on price alone. That's because most other countries don't carry all the baggage of health care costs, oil costs, and the entitlements

Table 1.4 China: Hourly Compensation Costs of Manufacturing Employees in China versus United States, 2002–2008

Year	(Chinese Currency: Yuan)	(US$) Equivalent
2002	4.74	0.57
2003	5.17	0.62
2004	5.50	0.66
2005	5.95	0.73
2006	6.44	0.81
2007[2]	8.06	1.06
2008	9.48	1.36

The accumulated evidence to date, including China's First National Economic Census, supports the general validity of the BLS annual calculations on China's manufacturing employment and labor compensation.

SOURCE: U.S. Bureau of Labor Statistics, available at www.bls.gov/fls/china.htm.

Table 1.5 Hourly Compensation Costs of Employees in Manufacturing in India, 1999–2005

Year	Mean Hourly Earnings in Rupees (hourly pay for time worked) [1]		Total Compensation Ratio [2]		Hourly Compensation in Rupees [3] = [1] × [2]		Exchange Rate: Rupees/ USD [4]	Hourly Compensation in USD [5] = [3] ÷ [4]	
	All Employees	Production Workers	All Employees	Production Workers	All Employees	Production Workers		All Employees	Production Workers
1999	20.68	15.97	1.423	1.423	29.43	22.72	43.06	0.68	0.53
2000	22.54	16.97	1.406	1.406	31.68	23.86	44.94	.70	.53
2001	23.77	17.57	1.416	1.416	33.65	24.88	47.22	.71	.53
2002	24.95	18.22	1.417	1.417	35.36	25.83	48.63	.73	.53
2003	26.58	18.98	1.417	1.418	37.68	26.91	46.59	.81	.58
2004	27.57	19.46	1.398	1.398	38.55	27.21	45.26	.85	.60
2005	29.10	20.06	1.375	1.376	40.02	27.60	44.00	.91	.63

SOURCE: U.S. Bureau of Labor Statistics, available at www.bls.gov/opub/mlr/2010/05/art1full.pdf.

16

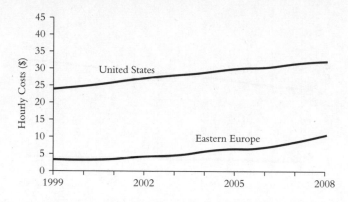

Figure 1.6   Hourly Compensation Costs in U.S. Dollars for All Employees in Manufacturing, Compared to Eastern Europe
Source: U.S. Bureau of Labor Statistics, "International Comparisons of Hourly Compensation Costs in Manufacturing, 2008," August 26, 2010, available at www.bls.gov/news.release/pdf/ichcc.pdf.

the United States hands out to workers. Workers in emerging countries don't expect entitlements; they just get to work and produce.

Let me tell you a true story. I met a guy named Hanz, who is a billionaire in the pharmaceutical industry. We were talking about a product he wanted to produce—a leg brace that makes it easier to walk without crutches. Hanz told me how he wanted to go into production

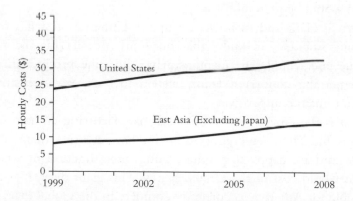

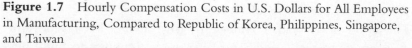

Figure 1.7   Hourly Compensation Costs in U.S. Dollars for All Employees in Manufacturing, Compared to Republic of Korea, Philippines, Singapore, and Taiwan
Source: U.S. Bureau of Labor Statistics, "International Comparisons of Hourly Compensation Costs in Manufacturing, 2008," August 26, 2010, available at www.bls.gov/news.release/pdf/ichcc.pdf.

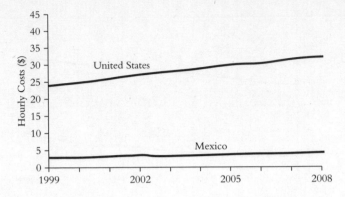

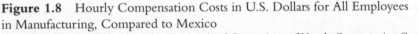

Figure 1.8   Hourly Compensation Costs in U.S. Dollars for All Employees
in Manufacturing, Compared to Mexico
Source: U.S. Bureau of Labor Statistics, "International Comparisons of Hourly Compensation Costs in
Manufacturing, 2008," August 26, 2010, available at www.bls.gov/news.release/pdf/ichcc.pdf.

and so I suggested he look into setting up a factory in Detroit. I said,
"You'll have lots of labor; people there are eager for jobs."

He wouldn't even consider it. He instantly jumped to the end game
and was looking at Vietnam, the Philippines, China, India, and Bangladesh because he could hire people there and not worry about health
care, employee benefits, sexual discrimination, or liability insurance.
In those countries the workforce was ready, willing, and able to do the
job and would be grateful for it.

Even if Hanz did manufacture in the United States, it would be
economic suicide. He knew that once his product hit the market,
someone else would start manufacturing the same product in one of
these emerging countries. Hanz needed to start out competitive in
order to remain competitive.

That is the current economic and manufacturing climate we find
ourselves in. These emerging countries have massive manufacturing
capacity and are happy to produce things for a fraction of what production would cost in the United States. This giant disparity makes it
impossible for America to currently compete in the global marketplace
and therefore we are losing jobs that won't come back.

The good news is that Americans have always been innovators
and have access to technology and have the brainpower to build new
industries and jobs.

The good news is that Americans have an inbred entrepreneurial spirit and where there are no jobs now, we can create new jobs and new industries to meet new needs.

We Have Used Up Our Grace Period

The iPhone is one of the greatest ideas in the last five years, maybe even the last 50 years. This amazing advance in how we communicate and exchange information is transforming people's lives. It carries a label saying "Made in China."

It used to be that when there was a technological breakthrough in the United States, whether it was the automobile, television, or airplane, there was a grace period where we had handled the manufacturing. We had time to create jobs and build prosperity. Then Japan overtook our automobile and television industries and those U.S. industries eroded. Next it was microwaves and small electronics. It happens over and over again. We would have the lead in manufacturing for a little while then production would go overseas. That lead no longer exists for the United States and it won't come back.

Over the years wages and health care costs have risen in the United States and increased the cost of production. Meanwhile China opened up with plenty of cheap labor and even inexpensive engineering and jobs went. Business margins improved and stockholders were happy.

No one really knows how many jobs have been outsourced outside of the United States, because companies are not required to disclose this information and so they never talk about it. Most economists agree that although the majority of the jobs are low-tech and production jobs, engineering and creative work is also going overseas. Here's what the Council for Foreign Relations has to say about the scope of this issue:

> Most estimates of U.S. jobs lost come from consulting companies or industry groups directly involved in outsourcing. Boston-based consultancy Forrester estimates that 400,000 service jobs have been lost to off-shoring since 2000, with jobs leaving at a rate of 12,000 to 15,000 per month, says John McCarthy, the company's director of research. Other estimates

say up to 20,000 jobs a month may be moving overseas. This is in addition to the 2 million manufacturing jobs that are estimated to have moved offshore since 1983.

(www.cfr.org/publication/7749/trade.html)

To give you an idea of just one industry that has been impacted, take a look at Figure 1.9, which appeared in the July 2010 issue of *BusinessWeek* in conjunction with an article by past Intel CEO Andy Grove.

As you can see, Figure 1.9 compares employee numbers for some well-known American technology corporations with those of Chinese technology corporation Foxxconn. Incidentally, in addition to producing its own products, Foxxconn produces items such as the Apple iPhone for these American tech firms.

When the next bright idea comes about, when the next Hanz wants to produce a product, those jobs will immediately go overseas. The United States won't even get the juice of that economic prosperity. We are quickly merging into one global economy, and if Americans expect to survive, we need to have a global clientele and some kind of parity in wages and realistic expectations.

The good news is that our wealth of technological know-how, entrepreneurial spirit, and intellectual resourcefulness gives our country an advantage when it comes to creating solutions to some of the

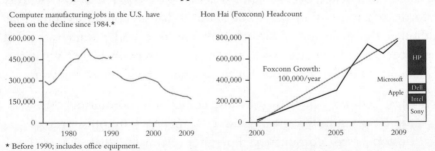

"Foxconn employs more than . . . Apple, Dell, Microsoft, HP, Intel, and Sony combined"

Figure 1.9   China Takes the Lead in Computer Manufacturing
Source: Bloomberg, *BusinessWeek*, July 2010. *Data Source:* Bureau of Labor Statistics; Thompson Financial Extel company reports.

most pressing challenges facing this planet. We've leapt ahead before and we can do it again.

We Produce Food That Impairs Our Health and Depletes Our Treasury

We were once the breadbasket of the world and now we are net importers of food. The food we do produce is saturated with toxins, antibodies, and hormones. This food is produced mainly by huge agriculture conglomerates and factory farms.

The agriculture conglomerates grow genetically altered grains that flourish under heavy doses of petrochemical fertilizers, which end up in the food that we eat and feed to our children.

The factory farms raise poultry, cows, pigs, and sheep on feed that is rich in hormones and antibiotics. According to the Union of Concerned Scientists, as much as 70 percent of all the antibiotics used in the United States are fed to healthy farm animals. (This information is taken from the Antibiotics section of "Sustainable Table," updated at www.sustainabletable.org/issues/antibiotics in October 2009.) I don't like to use the "conspiracy" word, but it seems the factory farms are generating big business for pharmaceutical companies.

Maybe these farms consider antibiotics preventative medicine, but it makes no sense to me. It's fairly common knowledge that when your body gets constant doses of antibiotics, it builds up resistance and then you need larger doses or stronger drugs to have any effect.

The synthetic hormones consumed by this livestock are also dangerous. An organization called MILK recently estimated that 30 percent of the milk cows in the United States may be treated with rbGH, which is a growth hormone (statistic from "Hormones in Food" by Rutuja Jathar). Furthermore, according to the National Cattlemen's Beef Association (NCBA), today more than 80 percent of U.S. cattle are raised using artificial hormones to increase their growth rate and body mass. In the larger feedlots, that figure is 100 percent (see www.buzzle.com/articles/hormones-in-food.html).

In addition, these artificial hormones, especially synthetic estrogen, showing up in our food, are also used entirely too casually in many over-the-counter products, and the effect on living creatures is not good. Here is a very simplified version of how these synthetic endocrine disrupters work.

Your body has receptors for lots of hormones including testosterone and a variety of estrogen hormones. Synthetic hormones mimic the real hormones; when they enter the body, they block the receptors so the natural hormones can't be absorbed. This negatively impacts your immune system by making it hard for your body to fight off viral and bacteria infections. It also has a serious impact on the reproductive ability of many creatures.

These endocrine interrupters have been associated with aberrations in reproductive organs of birds, otters, endangered Florida panthers, alligators, fish, and mollusks. Up and down the food chain, animals are exhibiting hermaphrodite features, low testosterone and low sperm count, and a general reduction in the number of their offspring. This information is documented in many publications such as the *Toxicology Letter, Journal of Clinical Endocrinology, Biochemical Pharmacology,* and *Environmental Health Perspective.* National speaker and author Betty Kamen, PhD, has also written extensively on the impacts of artificial hormones.

Now, as if the load of hormones we consume wasn't alarming enough, most of our food processing plants also seal up your cans and bottles of soup, beverages, baby food, and juice with a plastic resin sealant that contains Bisphenol A (BPA). While there is no direct evidence that BPA exposure adversely affects reproduction or development in people, hundreds of laboratory studies using rodents show that exposure to high dose levels of BPA during pregnancy and/or lactation can reduce survival, birth weight, and growth of offspring early in life. The test animals also showed earlier onset of puberty and an increased risk of obesity compared to unexposed animals. There is also significant evidence that even low doses correlate with negative effects (see http://cerhr.niehs.nih.gov/evals/bisphenol/bisphenol.pdf).

This isn't just a problem in the United States. In a separate report from the Food Standards Agency/Committee on Toxicity in the United Kingdom, BPA was shown to enlarge the prostate gland in laboratory mice, advance the onset of puberty in the females, and reduce fertility in rats. This agency also reported that the use of BPA is very widespread; BPA was found in nearly two-thirds of the canned foods tested, which included tuna, baked beans, and fruit cocktail. It is no wonder people are having problems with fertility and I won't even go into the impact of this stuff on the libido.

You need to understand that these fertilizer chemicals, antibiotics, and growth hormones do not break down. They are cumulative. They are stored in the environment, in the flesh of the animals we eat and then in our flesh. They are stored in the urine and manure that gets drained into our water supply.

We are seeing an epidemic of obesity and fertility problems as well as a significant rise in prostate and breast cancer. Most of these problems correlate with our increased consumption of chemicals, antibiotics, and hormones in our food. With so much of our food making us sick, it is no surprise that we are seeing an increased demand for food produced organically.

We Are What We Eat, Breathe, and Drink—and It Is Costing Us a Fortune

This nation spends $2.4 trillion on the concept of health and no one is getting any healthier! We're a nation of sick people. We are not only sick in our bodies, but we also are sick in our minds and sick at heart.

I believe that our health is a vital part of our wealth. Yet, we pay more attention to our investments and cars than to what we put in our bodies. We are doing so many things to undermine our health it's no wonder we have so much disease and that our health care costs are soaring. If we want to reduce our medical costs, we need to be accountable for our own health and treat our bodies with the same respect, if not more, that we give our car or our money.

The way we eat and the poor quality of our food sends us to the doctor for multiple problems from diabetes to obesity to vitamin deficiency. Our food is loaded with heavy metals, chemicals, and hormones that have been traced to any number of diseases and reproduction problems. All those problems cost money, which weakens our economy, depletes our treasury, and destroys the value of the dollar!

We are a culture that consumes fatty fast food as if it were air. It is ruinous to our health. Presently we spend more money in the United States on burgers than we spend on our space program to launch satellites and send rockets to the stars. It's a fact. NASA's 2009 fiscal year budgetary resources totaled $17.782 billion. In 2000, Americans spent over $110 billion on fast food. As of 2009, there were more than 25,000 fast-food chains, an increase of more than 1,000 percent since 1970, and now Americans spend more than $140 billion each year on fast food. The rise in obesity in this country correlates with this increased consumption of fatty fast foods. Add this to the general lack of nutrition in our food and we open the door to many medical problems and their related costs.

We Are Jeopardizing Our Life Support Systems

We are a planet with finite resources. Beyond the obvious mineral resources already used as global bartering chips, we have limited farmland, forests, wildlife, clean air, and clean water. Demand for these raw resources and for the basic necessities of life already outstrips supply. This adds to the tensions in the world, tensions that will continue to grow as more countries develop an appetite for our Western lifestyle.

The earth has only so much land and, barring some natural disaster, we aren't going to get any more. That makes what we have especially precious, but instead of treasuring the earth we abuse it. In our nation we plow under our farmland and build housing subdivisions and shopping malls we don't need. Then we string our houses and stores together with concrete roads that block rain from seeping into the ground, lowering our water tables, and affecting people and animals everywhere.

Huge agriculture conglomerates abuse massive tracts of land with assembly line farming and saturate the soil with fertilizers and pesticides that destroy natural organisms and threaten the health of people and wildlife.

We pollute our air. Companies and vehicles around the world literally spew tons of carbon dioxide from fossil fuel emissions into our atmosphere every day (see Table 1.6).

Table 1.6   U.S. Energy-Related Carbon Dioxide Emissions by Fossil Fuel

	Petroleum	Coal	Natural Gas	Total
	Million Metric Tons Carbon Dioxide			
1990	2,178	1,797	1,026	5,007
1995	2,206	1,894	1,186	5,296
2000	2,458	2,141	1,234	5,844
2001	2,469	2,084	1,185	5,740
2002	2,468	2,094	1,242	5,817
2003	2,513	2,131	1,209	5,864
2004	2,603	2,158	1,191	5,963
2005	2,620	2,161	1,179	5,972
2006	2,585	2,131	1,158	5,885
2007	2,568	2,154	1,234	5,967
2008	2,413	2,130	1,247	5,802

SOURCE: Energy Information Administration.

Between deforestation and the use of fossil fuels, carbon dioxide in the atmosphere has increased by 35 percent. Figure 1.10 is a chart of the increase of CO_2 in just the past 50 years.

Thousands of people end up dealing with respiratory diseases. A RAND study found that California's failure to meet federal clean-air standards cost $193 million dollars from 2005 to 2007. These costs are associated with 30,000 hospital admissions and emergency room visits.

An extra bonus from all this excess carbon dioxide in the air is a dramatic increase in acid levels in the ocean, due to the fact that the ocean acts as a huge sponge. Research and reports from several reputable sources show that in just the last 100 years our oceans have seen a 30 percent decrease in pH, about 100 times faster than any changes in ocean acidity in the last 20 million years; the current level of acidification is expected to more than double in the next 40 years, making it unlikely marine life will be able to adapt. This change in pH levels is already destroying marine life and our food chain. In Washington state we are reading about oyster beds that are no longer producing due to a decrease in pH levels in the water.

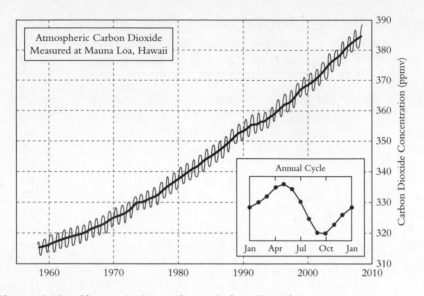

Figure 1.10 Changes in Atmospheric Carbon Dioxide
Source: Energy Information Administration.

We pollute our aquifers. Here's a good example: On the Potomac River in Washington, D.C., there are no fewer than seven cities and no fewer than seven sewage plants and no fewer than seven water uptake systems. They suck that water out of the river then use it for drinking and whatever and then expel it back into the river. The next town downriver sucks it up, drinks it, and expels it. And the next town does the same thing. And the next. And the next. All the way down the Potomac River. Lovely.

As if this wasn't enough, in 2005, Congress passed the Energy Policy Act, championed by then–Vice President Dick Cheney, which exempted a particularly destructive drilling practice called hydraulic fracturing from numerous long-held environmental regulations such as the Safe Drinking Water Act. Hydraulic fracturing, or fracking, is used in natural gas exploration.

This process involves pumping a cocktail of over 600 toxic chemicals and dozens of known carcinogens along with salt and sand into drilling holes. The mixture causes the shale to fracture and release natural gas. The big problem with this is that that chemical cocktail is ending up in the regional aquifers.

As I write this, a news clip video is playing on my computer that shows a man from northeast Pennsylvania turning on his kitchen faucet and then setting his water on fire with his lighter. Seriously! Gas was coming out of the faucet and big flames were burning right off the water. Do you want to drink that water? Do you want your hot water heater full of stuff that could blow up? This process is very widespread and YouTube has videos from Texas, Wyoming, Pennsylvania, and beyond. In September 2010, the EPA began holding hearings about the process and they expect massive public turnout. (For more information, see http://gaslandthemovie.com.)

Globally, we are racing to deplete our resources. We have emerging third-world countries crippled with debt that clear-cut and export their forests then use the barren land to grow poppies. This destroys habitat for thousands of creatures, erodes the barren land, and makes the population even more vulnerable and reliant on the drug trade. This is both irrational and unsustainable.

When we look around for ways we can transform the world economically, we have to take a serious look at how we treat our food sources, water sources, and our air, both globally and locally. It is in our national interest to be able to feed ourselves and in our global interest to ensure that people everywhere are able to lead healthy, productive lives and contribute to the world's wealth and happiness.

The good news is that, as citizens of the world, more of us are waking up to the damage we are doing to our life support systems and are becoming aggressive advocates for changes in practices that demean our planet.

Glenn Beck and Me, Talkin' 'Bout a Revolution

I want to tell you a story. In the spring of 2010, I was vacationing in Hawaii when I got a call from Glenn Beck asking me to join him on his television show in Los Angeles. He wanted to interview me. He'd heard me talk during an interview on CNBC and had invited me onto his show to ask me some questions.

So, Glenn flew me into Los Angeles and as I'm riding to the studio in the back of this luxury town car, driving past all these palm trees on these eight lane boulevards and seeing these huge hundred-foot bill-boards featuring *American Idol* hopefuls, I felt like I was on a different planet. I mean, it was very surreal. I'm a New York boy transplanted to Seattle and the whole California ambiance feels like a fantasy anyway, and here I am riding in a limousine to a television studio where I'm going to be interviewed by Glenn Beck. I literally felt like I was living in someone else's movie and that someone was going to jump out any minute and shout, "Cut!"

Anyway, I'd talked to Glenn on the phone before and seen his show. I knew his brain fired like a machine gun and that he'd be firing questions at me from every conceivable direction, and some unconceivable directions as well. I knew I'd have to be in hyper-drive to keep up with him.

I'd done plenty of radio shows, but I wasn't even going to pretend to myself that I was going to be able to keep pace with him. I was praying to be able just to keep up! Well, I also hoped that I'd be able to give a respectable account of myself, but I was willing to settle for surviving whole.

At any rate, I'm riding in the back of this limousine and scrib-bling like a maniac in a notebook, trying to capture every possible idea that might come up during my interview with Glenn. I'd been writing since I'd boarded the plane in Oahu and only had a few pages left in my notebook. I was on my second pen.

I was seriously mining every corner of my mind for everything I knew about the global economy and the American experience and Wall Street and society and change and current events and mob mentality and mob behavior and fear and greed and politics and flood and famine and hurricanes and earthquakes and the oil spill in the Gulf and our endangered environment and our endangered health and our endangered food and our endangered children and . . . well just about everything that might possibly relate to the mess the world is in.

I remember thinking particularly about Greece and about the building concern in the international community about how that country was going to extricate itself from imminent bankruptcy. This trip to Los Angeles was at least a full week before the riots in Greece and I, like many other people on the planet, was seriously concerned about what would happen in Greece, and then what would happen in all the other countries that were in similarly precarious economic situations due to their overwhelming debt. At that point in time, Greece looked like the first in a whole row of dominos just waiting for a breeze. Anyway, I was filling pages and pages of this stuff and it was . . . well, it was simply overwhelming.

Finally my brain just stopped. My pen just stopped. Time just stopped.

I just hovered. The surreal feeling expanded and I remember looking out the window and seeing yet another 200-foot billboard full of *American Idol* hopefuls flash by. Then a series of images flashed through my mind: Fire in the streets. People rioting. Gunfire. Bloody faces covered with bloody hands. Bloody bodies lying on the sidewalks. Cars overturned. Police in riot gear. Rifles. Smoke from tear gas. My images had no sound, but I could feel the sound of chaos. And I felt fear.

The pictures were as clear as any of the images that were beamed across the planet via satellite from the streets of Greece a few days later. But on that day, during my peaceful ride to the studio, Greece was just bubbling. None of those images had happened yet.

I'm not sure how long I sat, caught up in the images, but eventually I shook myself free and my pen attacked the page. I wrote one word. I wrote it in skyscraper-big capital letters at the bottom of the page. After sheets and sheets of notes I came to a single conclusion and I wrote one word. The word was REVOLUTION.

That was my conclusion. That was where I thought the world was headed. Revolution.

Don't think that idea didn't scare me, because it did. It would scare any sane person. But after processing everything I knew and projecting what I thought were likely outcomes, after recalling those images that had flashed through my brain, I concluded that we, the world, the economic system as we know it, was heading toward some kind of revolution. And that was what I wanted to say on Glenn's show.

I closed my notebook and put it away in my briefcase and enjoyed the rest of the ride through the surreal Los Angeles landscape.

A short time later the driver pulled into the studio lot and I was escorted past security and into the sound stage where Glenn would tape his show. Glenn's producer, Joe Kerry, greeted me and gave me a tour. He introduced me around to the crew and gave me a run down on what I might expect. At least, what he thought I might expect.

As Joe toured me through the studio I could hear Glenn calling out to his crew and the members of his team. Glenn is involved in every aspect of his show and if you've ever been in a television studio you know that there are a lot of things to be involved in. Glenn was all over the place and I could hear him calling out instructions about the lights, the props, the blackboards, the guests, the seating. He knew everything that was going on around him. Everything. I wouldn't be surprised to learn he could see through walls.

At one point he was talking to one of his crewmembers and I heard his voice rising as he talked about Greece. Then I heard him yelling, "It's all about Revolution! It's a revolution!"

I know it's a cliché, but I can't describe the feeling I had other than to say I literally felt a shiver run down my spine. A moment later I yanked my notebook out of my briefcase and flipped through the pages until I found what I wanted. I held the page up in front of Joe, pointing to the word I'd written after my montage of images. Glenn and I had reached the same conclusion. Revolution was on the horizon.

I don't recall much of the actual interview, but I do remember one point when Glenn held my notebook up to the camera for the viewers to see and pointed to my one-word conclusion to help him make his point. A few days later Greece experienced its meltdown and all those images I'd imagined during my limousine ride were flashed around the world on prime time television.

I can't believe that Glenn and I are the only people reaching this same conclusion. I mean, I'm smart and Glenn is smart, but there are a lot of smart people on the planet and I'm sure a lot of them are seeing the same writing on the same wall that Glenn and I saw.

But at the time of that show, no one was talking about Revolution. It was like the "F" word and not fit for prime time viewing. No one would talk about the New World Order either. Now, I listen to talk shows and it's like people are finally coming out of denial and seeing what is really happening. That is a good thing. We can't do anything about finding solutions to our problems if we don't even acknowledge the problems. So, on that day, Glenn and I talked about Revolution. And now in this book I'm talking about the New World Order. And just last week, I heard a prime time, mainstream CNN talk show host interview a British economist who actually spoke the words, "New World Order." So the dialogue is now open to the public and we need to talk about it to make it happen the way we want it to happen.

And that, my friend, is why I wrote this book. The Revolution doesn't necessarily require that we have blood and fire in the streets, but it does require that we deal with reality, accept that we are seeing a total game change in the world and take action to make sure that world is one we want to live in.

We Can Be an Ostrich or a Hero

As a nation we've never been in this place before; economically, ethically, morally, and spiritually, we are at a crossroads. As a nation, as a society, as part of a global community, as citizens of the world, we have a moral obligation to do everything we can to reclaim America and this earth for ourselves and the generations of all life to come.

It's immoral to pass the problems we've created on to future generations. The ONLY moral action we can take is to face the consequences of our past choices and change how we make our decisions. Those decisions must be guided by our moral compass that demands that we be fair to our fellow travelers on planet Earth.

The choices we make in the next days, in the next few months, in the next year will leave a legacy for generations to come. It's up to each one of us to decide how we want to be remembered. As a generation, as a society, we can go down in history as the self-indulgence generation that bankrupted the most powerful nation on earth.

Or we can be remembered as the generation that stepped up to the plate when things got tough and did whatever it took to correct the unsustainable consequences of poor past choices. We can be remembered as ostriches that lived in denial and refused to be accountable for the problems we created, or we can become heroes of the age.

The best news is that most people want to do the right thing. Hopefully, this book will provide you with plenty of ideas about what those right things are.

Chapter 2

We Need to End Our Dependent Lifestyle

Our current reality is the result of our past choices. Our future will be the result of our current choices.

This is a simple idea with profound implications. All the concerns I outlined in the previous chapter are the result of millions of decisions made by millions of people over thousands of days. The United States was not always in this pickle and it won't stay in this pickle.

Americans have hit bottom plenty of times and come back up. That's the signature of success. Just as we evolved from a British colony into an independent nation, just as we survived one of the most brutal civil wars the world has ever seen, just as we pulled ourselves up out of the 1930s Great Depression and the devastation of the Dustbowl years, we will find ways to overcome our current challenges.

The only time we fail is when we get knocked down and stay down. Any effort to get back up is a success. Americans have a long

33

history of getting back up after being knocked down, and I expect we can do it again. I believe we can get out of the hole we have dug for ourselves. It won't be easy. But then anything worth having is worth working for.

I know this is true. I've hit bottom a few times, and I don't just mean I lost my house and car, although that did happen, too. I'm talking about struggling to find food to eat. I'm talking about struggling to find a safe place to sleep. I'm talking about not knowing who to trust. I know about survival. I also know that it was damn hard to work my way back up to where I could respect myself and provide for my family. But it has been worth it. It has been totally worth all of the struggles, because I am a better man for the effort. I am a better husband and a better father for knowing the value of that effort. I also know that I'm not the only one who has gone through that kind of struggle and I know I won't be the last. Many of us are going through that struggle right now.

That's why I am writing this book. I'm hoping it will serve as a crash course to help all of you in the midst of your struggle. I'm hoping it will help those of you trying to figure out what to do next and next and next. I'm hoping to help those of you hunting for answers and frightened of making mistakes.

So, I'm laying out some truths as I see them, and hope they will help you see past the illusions that have trapped so many of us. My goal is to provide some perspective that will at least lessen your struggle.

We Need to End Our Dependence on Our Addictions

I think many of the debt problems I previewed in the previous chapter stem from our discontent and our need to find relief from that discontent. At a subconscious level many of us feel disconnected and unhappy, and to appease this unease we seek escape. We reach for a drink, a cigarette, maybe go out and play a few hands of poker, or hit the casino. Maybe we run down to the video store for the latest video or hit the shopping mall. Then the next time we feel discontented we do it again. We do it again and again until the practice becomes addictive. We become dependent on outside stimuli to ease our discontent.

So, why is our society so discontented that we seek outside sources to fill our longings?

I believe that the primary source of our discontent comes from the advertising media.

As a society, we have been brainwashed into believing that we are not good enough. The media bombards us with lies. It tells us that we aren't rich enough, pretty enough, successful enough, thin enough, or exciting enough. It tells teenage girls that they are somehow inadequate if they don't look like Christina Aguilera, Brittany Spears, or Lindsay Lohan. We are brainwashed to believe that we smell bad and look bad and are unappealing if we don't buy this deodorant, this toothpaste, or this shampoo.

We're told that if we aren't driving a Mercedes or an $80,000 BMW, (whether we can afford it or not), we're not really living to our full potential. The media tells us that if we don't have a 5-bedroom, 4,000-square-foot mansion with a swimming pool, we aren't living the American Dream. The media tells us that if we don't have members of the opposite sex hanging on our every word, we have no sex appeal.

None of these things are true. They are what the advertisers want us to believe to make us discontented with ourselves so they can sell us a solution. But you aren't broken! We all have bumps and bulges. We've all had bad breath and fragrant clothes on occasion. We've all been less than appealing to the opposite sex at times. We've all struggled to get that next promotion and felt a little tight in the pocketbook between jobs. That's life.

Those perfect lives and perfect people the media shows us are illusions. This is how the media sows our discontent. We have become enamored of this virtual reality and have been convinced that these ideals are attainable and that if we attain them then we won't feel discontented.

Collectively the media, specifically advertising, has systematically lulled us into our discontent with imbecilic television programming and psychologically sophisticated advertising messages that fill our heads with idealized images and ego-battering messages that convince us that we don't measure up unless we buy . . . something.

And so we buy. We buy new cars, fancy clothes, diet drinks, and medication for our erectile dysfunction. We buy whatever the advertisers promise will make us happier.

And we want to be happy now. We want instant gratification and instant escape from our discontent. So we hand over our credit cards for instant relief.

And our need for instant relief is costing us. As of July 2010, the Federal Reserve reported that the total consumer debt in the United States—*not counting mortgage debt*—was $2,418.9 billion dollars, which breaks out to an average of $8,600 for every man, woman, and child in the country. That's not every wage-earner; that's every person including your grandmother and your sister's new baby.

Granted, the Federal Reserve reports indicate that this debt has been falling for the past two years as people pay down their revolving consumer debt and use their ready cash to buy food and other essentials instead. But I strongly suspect this behavior is due to the overall economic downturn and people's uncertainty about jobs rather than due solely to some core change in our sense of self-worth or some miraculous elimination of our discontent. I believe the cause of our discontent is still in place.

The media has robbed us of our sense of identity and sense of self-worth. It has made us changelings in our own skin. We have become so fixated on how things should appear that we are willing to mortgage our own lives and the lives of our children in order to maintain those illusions.

Our reality is that we live beyond our means. It must stop. We must end our dependence on the media to tell us what can make us happy. We must end our dependence on easy credit to give us temporary respite from our sense of discontent.

We need to focus on the way things really are and live more realistic lives. We need to adjust our values and the value of things based on their truth and usefulness, rather than their appearance. We need to stop letting "the man behind the curtain" tell us . . . I mean, sell us what we are supposed to want.

Are those $90 court shoes going to magically give you the persona of that glamorous basketball star? Do you really need a Hummer to drive your kids to kindergarten? How about that designer suit or Rolex watch? Do they somehow make you more successful or more talented? They're just shoes! Something to put between your feet and the ground. What does it matter who made the clothes on your back? They're just clothes. They don't keep you warmer or better protected than the garments you can get at Value Village or the discount warehouse at the shopping mall.

Look, I know people need to buy certain things to function in the world, and for you that might mean high quality clothing or a good town car, because that is required of your profession. I'm just saying you should buy things for the right reasons and not because you've succumbed to the advertising manipulation. Buy it because it actually adds value to your life, not because someone says it does.

At the same time, I don't mean to offend people by implying that everyone is spending money on frills that they can blithely cut from their budget. Many of us already live a fairly Spartan lifestyle, either by choice or through a serious change in our finances. I understand that many of us would happily sell our car or the kid's bunk beds if it would put food on the table, provided we still have a car or a bed to sell.

According to recent Gallup research, overall self-reported discretionary spending in stores, restaurants, gas stations, and online by upper-income Americans averaged between $107 and $121 a month. For middle- and lower-income consumers that monthly average is between $52 and $61. As low as these figures are, they are still down 20 percent since October 2009, which correlates with significant shifts in the employment expectations of many Americans.

We need to remember who we are. We are not defined by the advertising media. We are defined by our own beliefs and our own actions. We don't need to depend on some twenty-something comedy writer in Los Angeles for a reality check of what it means to be accepted, sexy, and successful. We need to stop depending on other people and other things outside of ourselves to bring us contentment, to fill that longing we have to "measure up" to some ideal standard.

We Need to End Our Dependency on Our Credit Cards

As a nation we have allowed banks and credit card companies to enslave us, enabling us to live irresponsibly. We have become dependent on our credit cards and we need to sever that addiction. Like any addiction, the first step is admitting that you have a problem. Once you take that first of seven steps you can't go back to ignorance. Making that admission can be painful and challenging, but it must be done. By you.

1. You need to decide that being crippled by monthly payments no longer serves you.
2. You need to release your attachment to things you can't pay for.
3. You need to train yourself to pay cash or walk away.
4. You need to decide to master the momentary impulses that urge you to rack up those thousands of dollars in credit card debt.
5. You need to recognize when you are susceptible to sales pitches or media manipulation.
6. You need to end the codependency between you and your credit card.
7. You need to destroy or limit your credit cards.

You can burn your card, cut it up, bury it, or perform some other ritual. Maybe you could have a credit card burning party and invite all the neighbors. You could call everyone and set a time to meet in the street and yell, "Debt is no longer my master" and burn the dang things. Then you could put it on YouTube and really start an avalanche of change! I'd like to see that!

I can hear some of you screaming at me. "Are you nuts? I need my credit to run my business!"

Look, I'm a pragmatist. I'm not talking about the credit businesses need to maintain inventory. That kind of credit is part of the business cycle. Face it, 70 percent of our GDP is based on retail industries that rely on credit to rotate their inventory. I'm talking about our irresponsible use of personal consumer credit. I'm talking about buying what we can't afford based on our wants rather than our needs.

Say "No" to the installment plan. Repeat after me: "My life is not an installment plan. My life and the lives of my family and children are too important to just break up into a series of easy payments."

We need to return to the values of our grandparents and parents. They didn't have credit. Their ethic was to pay as you go. Pay cash and only buy what you can pay for and watch prices fall. Prices are driven up because merchants know we can get credit and so they pump up the price. We've just been through this in the real estate bubble. Sellers will sell at the price the market will buy at. If the market perceives the value is more, they will pay more. With real estate that was easy to do because there were thousands of mortgage brokers willing to give buyers easy access to money in the form of mortgage loans, a form of credit. The more money available, the more the seller could ask for. If there is no credit—if we pay cash—then we'll see prices fall. We need to retrain ourselves to pay cash or walk away.

We Need to End Our Dependence on Unsustainable Entitlements

Right now our government enables the unemployed with up to 99 weeks of benefits. That's two years of no motivation and no incentive to get a job! It is also a huge leap from where unemployment benefits were.

In 1991, the Emergency Unemployment Compensation program allowed up to 13 weeks of federally funded unemployment benefits. In February of 1992, that was amended to allow 20 to 33 weeks in states with high unemployment rates and from 13 to 26 in all other states. In 2002, people unemployed due to the terrorist attacks could claim benefits for 26 to 39 weeks. In July 2008, an Emergency Unemployment Compensation program added an additional 7, then 13 weeks to eligible claims. This was good until June of 2009, but the jobs kept shedding. In early 2010, this was extended to 99 weeks.

Currently, states share part of the burden for these entitlements and they are seriously feeling the strain. According to several well-researched articles on ProPublica.org and supported by statistics from the Bureau of Labor, the demands of federal unemployment claims have pushed the unemployment insurance funds of 27 states into the red with 40 more states projected to go broke.

That entitlement program adds to our government debt and is unsustainable. Not only do these entitlements deplete our country's financial reserves, they undermine the motivation we need to create new ways to make money, to build new businesses, and to start new industries. Our government needs to give workers a hand up, not a hand out.

Don't get me wrong. Losing your main income is a real shocker. Nearly everyone has been there at one time or another; I certainly have. It's ugly. It's demeaning. It's humiliating to apply for work you're overqualified for or a job that is much less than you deserve. So having a buffer of unemployment insurance benefits is a real help while we're reeling from the shock. But it draws out the pain.

The need to rebuild our job base obviously needs to be a priority in this country. Eventually, workers have to find work. They have to find ways to put food on the table. Yet, the longer they postpone that truth, the easier it is to fall into a victim mindset. The longer people remain locked into living off the state, the harder it is to come back to feeling like a productive, valuable human being. It's insult on top of injury.

When people are focused on how to stretch their benefits, and how to apply for jobs that aren't there, they are not putting their minds to work to come up with ways to take care of themselves. This country is filled with smart, industrious people who know how to get things done. Yet the unemployment insurance system seems stuck in neutral and people are not motivated to do much more than coast.

I'm not saying unemployment insurance benefits are a bad thing. Only that the government needs to rethink the idea that slapping a bandage on a gushing wound is going to take care of the pain.

As a society we have also become dependent on Social Security and Medicare entitlements, which I discussed in the previous chapter. Personally, I think of these entitlements as something we should need to earn. Looking around at what we've done to our environment and to our economy, and looking at the massive debt we've left to our children and their children, I'm not sure we deserve anything back. I'm not sure that we've earned it.

Some of the best times I ever had were with my great-grandmother, Katherine Angell. I relished and valued every second I got to be in her presence. I felt honored and privileged to listen to her tell me about North Carolina and how Arcadia National Park was formed. I didn't care what she told me. I enjoyed it.

I owe her my respect, gratitude, and honor for all she gave me. But now, I am becoming older and at some point, I, too, shall become a senior citizen. And I look at myself in the mirror and ask, "Will I deserve the respect, gratitude, and honor of my children?"

How do you answer that question? Have you earned the respect and gratitude of your children?

Sadly, many of us cannot say we have earned it. Unless we take action and correct our errors, unless we do everything we can to fix the things on this planet that we have broken, unless we take drastic action to leave a healthy world for our children, then our children should not respect us. They should curse us.

So how can we make amends? How can we reduce the financial burden on our children? How can we repair the damage we've done to our environment?

The Social Security safety net is another entitlement program we have become dependent on. The only way I see that we can become less dependent on it is to not take our benefits if we don't need them. There are many people in this country who do not need to rely on Social Security to survive and I think they should seriously consider not claiming those benefits. The people who do need that help will already burden the system enough.

Another way we can reduce the drain on our treasury is by reducing our need for medical care. Our current technological prowess allows us to hook people up to intravenous feeds and heart–lung machines to keep them alive while the medical industry devours them one dollar at a time. This is sick. We must stop this momentum and learn to honor the life cycle as it was intended to be honored. We need to stop interfering with the natural cycle of life and death.

If we want to reduce medical costs, we must become proactive about taking care of our bodies. We must eliminate the root causes of our poor health and focus instead on creating good health. We must stop poisoning ourselves with toxins from fertilizers and pesticides. We must stop consuming hormones along with our beef and poultry. We must take drastic action to make the food production industry accountable for making us sick.

Let me tell you a story. There was a river that ran through a village. One year after a heavy rain the people in all the villages downstream started to get sick. In village after village, people were getting sick and dying. Finally, a group of villagers explored upstream and found a large elk, dead and caught on a tree snag and rotting as it floated in the water. The villagers pulled the elk out of the water and people stopped getting sick. They started being healthy and happy again. All they had to do was remove the cause of the bacteria that was making people sick. They just had to pull the rotting elk out of the water.

If America wants to be healthy, we need to eliminate the root causes of disease. I don't mean funding the race for the cure. There is no cure. There is only a cause. I believe that most of our illnesses are the result of extreme imbalances in our natural systems because of the amount of chemicals and hormones we routinely consume with our food and water. We need to eliminate these imbalances. We need to take the elk out the river. Then shall we be healthy and then shall our $2.4 trillion annual health care bill decline.

We Need to Stop Depending on the Government to Tell Us What Is Healthy

Here's crazy. You send your kid to camp with a can of mosquito spray. This stuff kills mosquitoes. Mosquitoes are biological creatures. Your kid is a biological creature. What do you think that does to his nervous system? His blood? His heart? We have been brainwashed into believing that if a product is on the store shelf that must mean that it's good. That is not what it means. It means that the Food and Drug Administration (FDA) ran tests and the stuff passed the tests. Those tests are whatever the FDA wants them to be. Use your common sense. If bug spray kills bugs, it can't be good for other biological creatures like your kid. The fact that it's on the shelf just means that the FDA is full of fools.

And have you noticed how many pharmaceutical ads are on television these days? I think these ads should be prohibited just like tobacco and hard liquor ads are. Just because these products are advertised on television does not make them safe. I see these ads and listen to how they're going to make my life better, then I listen to the side effects. I'm sorry, I don't think I want to risk blindness or hearing loss just so I can spend some quality time with my wife. We need to use our common sense instead of just trusting the bureaucracy to keep us safe.

Here's more craziness. My wife was on birth control pills for a few years. It was terrible. Those hormones interfere with every system in the female body and yet they are prescribed for everything from acne to convenience. This powerful hormone is saturating our biosphere and has been linked to any number of reproductive problems in species around the world, including humans. I'll get into that elsewhere.

We Need to End Our Dependence on Imported Energy and Fuels

The United States is a net importer of oil. That means we pay other countries to produce oil that we consume. That's because we don't produce enough of our own oil—or enough of our other fuels, either. The end result is that we are adopting more extreme measures to produce our own natural gas and oil and we are seeing a huge cost associated with those efforts. We cannot separate environmental concerns from our economic concerns. They are fully linked.

For example, we need oil, so we do more offshore drilling. Normally, the risks are contained, but then we have a sudden catastrophe and an oil gusher starts to despoil the Gulf of Mexico. Think about all the economic costs this entails. What is the number on the check to remediate the damage to the seafood industry in the Gulf? What is the number on the check to remediate the future damage to the ecosystem as this toxic sludge buries the life on the bottom of the ocean and destroys the bottom of our food chain? No check is large enough. As we allow our environment to be destroyed, we are damaging a portion of our food industry now and into the future.

The same kind of thing is happening in our natural gas industry. Politicians took advantage of our panic over our inability to supply sufficient fuel for ourselves. They circumvented key EPA rulings that protected areas of the nation from natural gas exploration. Once the doors were open, natural gas exploration firms began conducting a drilling practice called hydraulic fracturing, or fracking. I already explained how this damages our water supply. So far, about 45 percent of our aquifers have been impacted or are at risk. That's almost half!

What is the number on the check to fix half of the nation's aquifers? What is the number on the check to replace the elk, bears, raccoons, birds, fish, and people that will die of poison from that water?

The multitrillion-dollar debt our government has already racked up to keep dying industries on life support and pay bonuses to criminals, the multitrillion-dollar debt our government has already racked up to pay for a health care system that keeps dying people on life support and keeps the bank accounts of the big pharmaceutical companies plump, even these huge numbers can't come close to the multi-gazillion-dollar price tag for fixing our environment in the wake of our addiction to oil and natural gas.

I don't even think we have a number that big! Once we break our environment, we can't fix it. I'm sorry. We are racing downhill toward our own demise—both economically and environmentally, because environmental demise is the same as an economic demise. If we kill our environment, we kill our wealth; when you're dying of terminal cancer your money isn't worth much.

We Need to Reduce Our Dependent Prison Populations

Let me take a moment to talk about another kind of dependence that is a serious issue in the United States. Compared to the rest of the world, the United States has one of the largest prison populations as a percentage of the general population. And that population is expanding.

I believe that drug convictions make up a vast number of cases that end up in jail. But that doesn't stop the drug trade. If someone wants drugs, he or she can still get some even if their dealer goes to jail. When we put a body in jail, another body takes their place on the street. Obviously jail is not enough of a deterrent, so we need to try something else. I propose we decriminalize the use of some substances and get to the root causes of habitual drug use rather than just dealing with the symptoms.

What is causing these people to fall out of society? What has instilled in them such a lack of respect for themselves and others that they steal property and lives and sell drugs that kill?

I believe that one of the root causes of drug use, alcohol use, gambling, and other addictions is our need to escape. The root question we need to ask is: What are we trying to escape from? This epidemic of escapist behavior is a strong signal and symptom of a society that is not working. When life lacks value and purpose, then people have no compass and their life has little meaning or balance. If values and purpose are not instilled in us early, then we can drift endlessly from one short-term thrill to the next short-term thrill.

Every criminal was once a 3-year-old boy or a 4-year-old girl. As members of society, we must assume some of the responsibility for their crimes, because as a society we have not created an environment that provides those people with strong values and clear purpose. So, that is the solution to the root problem.

But that doesn't address the current expanding prison population and the increased costs related to incarcerating that population. CNNMoney reports that the United States incarcerates more people than any other country in the world, creating a $37 billion prison economy that is expanding day by day. More than two million inmates are currently serving time in U.S. prisons, up from 744,000 in 1985. And incarceration doesn't work. A 2002 statistical study by the Federal Bureau of Justice found that 52 percent of released convicts were back in jail within three years.

I wonder if there isn't some incentive in going to jail. Let's see. I get locked up for a few years, I get three square meals a day, a place to sleep, showers and medical care and access to a library so I can study for my law degree. Hmm? That doesn't sound like much of a deterrent to committing a crime. In fact, that probably sounds pretty good to the millions of people living on the street right now. Just think, as that prison population ages, they'll be getting free medical care at the taxpayer's expense.

This is an unsustainable situation. We must find ways to break this cycle and get these people out of jail, rehabilitated, and functioning in society. The incentive of the prison industry is not unlike that of the medical industry; one wants to keep you sick and the other wants to keep you locked up. That's sick.

Chapter 3

The Truth and Spin about the Pending Economic Meltdown

Everyone is talking about the declining U.S. dollar, the U.S. deficit, and the problems in other countries with excessive debt. Many people are talking about the likelihood of a significant economic meltdown. But no one is talking realistically about what that meltdown might entail. I think that is partly because it is too scary to contemplate, partly because no one wants it to happen.

I believe we will see an economic reset on a global scale. The current levels of insolvency among Westernized nations are unsustainable. We will see a reset that dissolves the rules currently governing international economics and forces a complete economic and social restructuring on the planet. I'm talking about a reset that will result in a New World Order.

The truth is that this reset is just over the horizon, but until it happens, people will continue to deny it, avoid thinking about the aftermath, and generally pretend that things are going to be okay. And that is fine with the powers that be, because they don't want the citizens of any nation to look too closely at what is really happening.

Why No One Wants to Talk About Why Our Deficit Cannot Be Repaid

Our current currency system is based on unsound money. By sound money I mean currency that is based on hard assets like gold, palladium, silver, or some other tangible commodity.

A U.S. dollar is a unit of measurement, and that measurement is based on the standard weight of silver. According to the 1792 Coinage Act, one single U.S. dollar bill equals 0.77344 ounces of silver. That was sound money.

If you look at the period between 1800 and 1941, inflation did not exist while the currency was sound. There was no such thing as inflation. Things cost what they cost based on supply and demand. Transactions were conducted using currency based on a fixed standard and prices remained fairly stable.

Also, the average consumer didn't have access to a lot of personal credit. They could save, pay as they went, or perhaps arrange a small loan with a bank or start a credit line with the grocer. There was no extra "unsound" money or access to excessive credit to allow for artificial inflation. So there wasn't any.

In 1971, President Nixon ended the practice of basing transactions on sound money. Immediately both the deficit and inflation took off like a rocket. Then Madison Avenue and the credit card companies got together and targeted consumer psychology and trained everyone over the age of eight to become a voracious consumer, and we never looked back.

This is why I believe that any discussion of our economic woes that doesn't address the need for sound money is a waste of time.

Someone sent me an e-mail that provided an excellent example of the value of using sound money. According to mercantile records written in the Bible between 450 and 425 b.c. (2 Chron 1:17), you could buy a horse for 150 shekels of silver.

Do the math.

Multiply 150 shekels at 11.5 grams of silver each, where every 1,725 grams equaled 60.85 ounces of silver. This was the equivalent of $1,110.51 in today's dollars, or at least as of July 13, 2010.

A shekel is worth 11.5 grams of silver.

Multiply 150 shekels at 11.5 grams of silver each and you get 1,725 grams of silver.

1,725 grams of silver is equal to 60.85 ounces of silver.

As of July 13, 2010, silver was going for around $18.25 per oz.

Multiply $18 times 60.85 and you get $1,095.30 in today's dollars.

I know you can still get a horse for around $1,000, so think about that. In the 2,500 years since the bill of sale for that horse was recorded, there has been no inflation. That's because they were using sound money based on a fixed weight of silver.

Let's look at a more recent example. In 1950 you could buy a gallon of gas for $0.18. Now, $0.18 times 0.77344 equals 0.139219 ounces of silver to buy a gallon of gas. As of July 13, 2010, the price of silver is $18.25 per ounce. If you multiply $18.25 times 0.139219 you get $2.54. What is the price of a gallon of gas today? Hmmm?

So, between 1950 and 2010 we see very little actual increase in the cost of gas if you are paying with silver. My point is that the cost of gas, milk, and many other goods has not changed significantly in terms of sound money. It is only the value of the unsound dollar that really changes, and it only changes because the dollar no longer represents a fixed weight.

Makes you think, doesn't it? If we get rid of all the extra dollar bills, settle down to a fixed number of dollars or some other unit of exchange that correlate with the actual amount of silver or gold or some other precious metal, then we could be dealing again with sound money. Maybe the price of things would become more realistic based on their true value and the true value of our currency.

With sound money a government has to actually have the money to spend it. With unsound money the government can print as many dollar bills as they want, the only restraint being that the money they print represents inflation and a debt to be paid to the Federal Reserve for doing us the favor of printing the money.

Did you catch that? We have to repay the Federal Reserve a debt amount that is equal to the face amount of each Federal note (what we call a dollar today), plus interest.

Plus interest? We have to pay interest to the Federal Reserve for the money they print?

Yes, we do. That's one of those pesky little details no one bothers to teach us in our country's outstanding educational system. In fact, our nation's educational system seems determined to avoid teaching anyone about anything that has to do with how our money and financial system works. But that is another topic for another time.

Anyone who understands the money supply knows that there are not enough actual dollars in existence to pay off the deficit, because of this "plus interest" factor. To give you an idea of the scope of this problem, look at what we've been paying in interest on the national debt:

In 1990, it was $264,852,544,615.90.
In 2000, it was $361,997,734,302.36.
In 2010, it is $375,247,863,222.70.

According to several economists, at this rate it is only a matter of a few years before the interest payments will outstrip the original debt.

No one is talking about controlling the deficit under the current system, because it is impossible. It's like we're constantly trading on margin and assuming we'll never get a margin call and never have to repay what we borrowed. As long as we are servicing the interest payments on all the money the Fed is printing, as long as we are servicing all the loans we've taken out to buy our own debt, as long as we're servicing all the loans we've taken to underwrite our entitlements. . . . Well, you get the idea.

After learning this, it can come as no surprise to you to learn that the United States loses money every day. That's the other half of this impossible situation.

The United States cannot maintain its current economic condition. The United States is basically bankrupt and constantly losing money. Every day that the United States is open for business, globally, we are running in the red paying interest on the money we've borrowed from other countries, from our own Federal Reserve, and from our children. Today, yesterday, last month, last year, for the last decade, the United States has been running in the red.

Obviously, our circumstances are not sustainable. I think we will see the end of this situation in a bankruptcy sale. The United States will eventually have a bankruptcy sale and work it out with our creditors. Large segments of the U.S. economy will be sold to buyers around the world and we will lose ownership of vast segments of the economy to the Chinese, the Middle East, and the Russians, because they have the money.

Where did they get the money? From us, of course!

We send over $800 billion per year overseas to buy oil. Now those countries have the money and we have the debt and nothing left to sell. We have already cut down vast segments of our forests. We can't expand our mineral mining unless some creative politician manages to strong-arm the EPA into cutting some back-room deal to let corporations mine for natural gas in Yosemite and Yellowstone. And no, that is not a suggestion! They're trying!

The bottom line is there will need to be a reset button on the U.S. deficit. The only good aspect of this situation is that most of the other nations are also in a pickle and probably won't put up tremendous resistance, because a reset for the United States will mean a reset for them, too. I'll talk more about what that reset might look like in Chapter 6 about the time line for the crash of the U.S. dollar.

If you think about it, the dollar is like a share of common stock in a company where the United States is the company. If people are enthusiastic about the company and news is good, then share prices rise. If people are worried and the company has bad news, then its share price falls. Now, add debt to the mix. If a company has a lot of debt, then when the stocks fall they tend to go lower than they would in response to just the news. It's sort of an added bonus.

How does this relate to bankruptcy and resets? The movement of the U.S. dollar reflects the degree of faith people have in the U.S. government. Those dollars represent a promise that they are backed with the full faith and promise of the government. The fact that the dollar's value is falling reflects a lack of faith in the U.S. government. It's a rejection by other nations of the validity of the U.S. government, a rejection of that full faith and promise, and a rejection of the U.S.

economic system. We are seeing nothing less than a rejection of the status quo and it is playing out on a global stage.

But it is also a rejection by U.S. citizens of the relationship between the people and their elected officials. That is because the U.S. government that was built by the people and for the people no longer exists. The government we now have was built by the government for the government.

This reckless self-indulgence by the U.S. government is angering millions of people in this country and all around the planet. We have not been living in harmony with our neighbors. Since our government is merely a reflection of the values we have allowed to rule us, as Americans living a self-indulgent lifestyle, we must accept that we deserve that anger and start to make amends.

The Truth about Tariffs and Jobs

The United States is losing its jobs to other countries and we think that slapping tariffs on imported goods will level the playing field. It won't. The jobs we have lost are production jobs and they have been shipped overseas to places where people do production for a fraction of what it costs to produce in the United States.

Okay. That's easy to understand.

What people don't understand is that adding a tariff to imports won't bring the jobs back. They are gone.

I'm sorry, but the jobs that went away aren't jobs filled by chip scientists, semiconductor engineers, or physicists. They are jobs that were filled by regular folk who drink Budweiser and watch baseball in the evening. The mothers are in the PTA and the dads coach Little League teams. On weekends the families go to church and play Bingo. These are America's blue-collar workers. Their jobs are gone and tariffs are not going to bring them back.

Here's why.

U.S. workers look at their jobs leaving the country and say, "We want those jobs back, but we also want our benefits and our pensions. And since we insist on our benefits, we can't compete with Mexico, the Philippines, China, Bangladesh, and Vietnam; so we want tariffs to make their products more expensive and give us a fair and level playing field."

I should add that it isn't just the U.S. middle-class worker saying this. We hear the same thing from the French, the Greeks, and the Italians. But no one can compete with Mexico and Vietnam because of the wage disparity. Those countries don't pay out millions of dollars in workers' benefits like the United States, France, Greece, and Italy do.

So we put up barriers in the form of tariffs in an effort to protect our industries. I agree that it is important to protect our industries, but when you are talking about global trade and global commerce, there is no way to do that, not as long as workers insist on all these costly benefits.

To get an idea of how much of our money goes to pay for benefits, take a look at Figure 3.1, the International Labor Comparison chart for 2010 from the Bureau of Labor Statistics. Hourly compensation includes basic wages plus benefits and other pay. In 2006, Norwegian factory owners paid employees an hourly average of $41.05 with $27.54 going to wages and $13.51 for benefits and other pay.

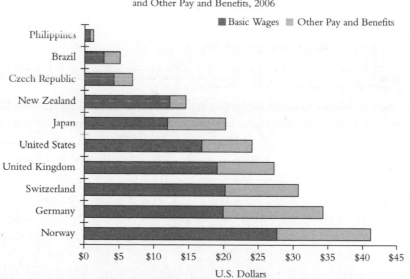

Figure 3.1 International Labor Comparison Chart
Source: U.S. Bureau of Labor Statistics.

Compare that with the Philippines for that same year. Those workers averaged $1.07 an hour, with $0.80 for wages and $0.27 for benefits and other pay. While the United States is pretty much in the middle of this particular chart, it is still easy to see that our benefits and other pay add a big chunk to our average hourly wages with about $18 going to wages and $5 going to benefits and other pay for an average hourly wage of about $22.50 for 2010.

In the global arena, businesses operate on the premise of *the survival of the fittest*. That means the industry that can produce and sell the goods at the cheapest price is going to survive and the others won't. Tariffs may buy some time, but they can't save an industry that is not competitive.

Let me give you an example. Say you produce rice in your country and there is another country that can produce rice at half the cost. Now that other country exports their rice into your country. They are able to produce it for 50 percent of what it costs you and therefore they can sell it for a lot less. Now, say your country wants to make the price of the imported rice roughly comparable to the price of your domestic rice, so they slap an extra fee on it.

From the consumer's standpoint, they like to be able to buy goods at the lowest possible price. But now all the rice costs the same—at the higher price—so the consumer doesn't benefit. It doesn't matter to them if they buy domestic or imported rice. They'll buy based on other factors, like taste or availability, or packaging or habit.

The truth is that at the end of the day, tariffs don't work because all it does is freeze up the global economy.

If you are a capitalist and believe in the capitalist system with free trade and free markets, if you believe in the law that supply inevitably meets demand, if you believe in pricing goods for about what they are worth, if you believe in the efficiency of markets, then you know that tariffs, restrictions, and government regulations never work.

However, if you are a socialist and if you want big government control, then tariffs give you the illusion of control. Plus, they sound good to those disgruntled workers holding out for all those jobs that aren't coming back.

The truth is that markets must find their own course and level. Economies, markets, and industries are always in a state of birth, maturation, aging, and destruction. Just like people. These cycles are a natural part of economics, and the law of supply and demand requires that industries disappear to be replaced by new industries.

Adding tariffs to "level the playing field" is just a delaying tactic. We don't want to delay the inevitable. We don't want to draw out the pain. We want a fast, deep cut so we can start healing. We don't want our workers to be holding out for jobs in dying industries that will never come back. We don't want a generation of obsolete workers for obsolete industries. We want those workers to be available for new industries. The sooner we stop resisting the coming change, the sooner we stop trying to control the markets with tariffs, and the sooner those new industries can start developing.

Big Corporations Spin the Truth and Play Down the Problems They Cause

Distrust of big business is rampant and justified. Like governments, corporations seek to survive into perpetuity. They say it is for the benefit of the shareholders and investors and that's good, because investors want their investments to expand. But in order to do that, the corporations must profit. So they play down any problems that might interfere with their profits. They say the right things to the media, pay off the right politicians, and award big bonuses to their executives for hiding the truth. The shareholders get their dividends and everyone is happy.

That is, until the corporation is found to be poisoning the water in a region and people and animals die. Or it's discovered that the corporation bypassed safety measures at a production site and an oil rig blew up and people died and an entire ecological region is undermined. Then shareholders and other people are outraged because they didn't know about the damage these corporations were doing in order to generate those dividends.

So, how can big business like these corporations get away with spinning their lies and bulldozing people?

You have to understand that we have two different classes of people. We have the economic elite and then we have the rest of the world. Only the rest of the world doesn't count, because we're just a bunch of people and animals and oceans and stuff. Nothing important.

Increasingly, because of the disparities of wealth on a global basis, corporations are being run by this minority of financially powerful elite. This is a small group of influential economic elite who have nearly limitless power. They are not elected, yet they control who is elected. They have no legal standing, but apparently they have considerable influence as evidenced in the recent U.S. Supreme Court ruling to allow unlimited corporate contributions to campaigns. They are not hired, but they hire lobbyists. They are not answerable to anyone, but they own the 10 major media conglomerates that tell 309 million Americans what to think. They own multinational corporations that can endlessly protect themselves while they exert control and influence around the globe.

I'd like to know what kind of pressure these big businesses put on the U.S. Supreme Court to sway those judges into removing the limit on how much money corporations can contribute to political campaigns. I'd also like to know why we heard nothing about this change until after it was signed into law and announced on national television during the evening news. When was this change proposed? How did it get to the Supreme Court without anyone reporting on it? How long was it deliberated? Who were the supporters and who said nay? Where were the reporters? They should have been all over that! This change in the law is tantamount to inviting the fox inside the henhouse and saying, "Dig in!"

This is the kind of back-room power play the economic elite and their powerful corporations specialize in. This is the same kind of end run made by the lobbyists to get the restrictions on hyrofracking waived, which has resulted in tainting nearly half of the nation's aquifers. These corporations have become so voracious and so consumed with expansion at any cost that they run rampant over things like the environment and constitutional rights.

Then if the media catches them, they play down the problems they create and use their influence to sway politicians and use their own media to give it a good spin, or bury the story entirely. Sure, a few people might get cancer from the pesticides in their food and a few houses might explode when their water tanks fill up with natural gas, and a few hundred aquatic species might become extinct because they can't live in our acidified oceans, but these are minor blips on the radar for these powerful behemoths. As long as the bottom line stays in the black and the shareholders get their dividends, the rest of the world can go hang. And it is hanging, as evidenced by the rise in the number of cancer cases around the world and the growth in the health care industrial complex.

In addition to exploiting resources for their own profit, many multinational corporations also exploit workers and argue that they are improving the quality of life for those workers, especially in third world nations. At some level that may be true, but on another level I know it is just their spin to justify exploitation for profit.

I have to ask how fair and equitable is it to have some 8-year-old kid in the Philippines living in a sewer making $140 dollar sneakers for some 8-year-old kid in France or Germany? How fair is that? If we brought the parents of both of those kids together and they talked about trading the sweat of one child for the pleasure of another child, what would they determine is fair? The truth is that the 8-year-old worker and his family are probably extremely grateful for the income, because that family needs the money in order to eat. But is it fair?

Here is the real question we need to ask: Are corporations the enemy?

To the extent that corporations act in a manner that is against the common good in exchange for profits to the shareholders, then yes, I would say that immoral corporations probably are the enemy; or at least a primary one among a field of enemies. But I believe these immoral corporations are just a vehicle for the economic elite who are the true power behind global economics.

If you want to read more about what this elite is in the United States, some expert investigative journalists from the *New York Times* and the *Wall Street Journal* are following several stories for ProPublica.org.

We need to stop them. We need a call to action to take on the powerful corporations and force them to stop their unsustainable practices.

Our migration toward self-reliance and sustainable lifestyles must include strong social action. It is imperative that each one of us step out of our comfort zone and do something. Maybe that is writing a letter to your Congressman or Congresswoman. Maybe it's writing a letter to the editor of your local paper. Maybe it's following the town hall schedule and claiming your 15 minutes to propose some change.

Pick a cause and get involved. We need a social uprising that hits these conglomerates and this club of economic elites in the pocketbook. We need a battalion of outraged global citizens to demand an end to bailouts and sweet deals for corporate industries that should be allowed to die. We need to erode the power of immoral corporations that are controlling governments and destroying our planet. That is why I pray that the New World Order, should it come into being, include powerful and enforceable policies to prevent this kind of financial pressure.

The American Dream Has Turned Nightmarish

The corporate model we have created is dedicated to chasing what we call the American Dream. People are now realizing that, in chasing this illusion, we have created a dysfunctional economic system and self-indulgent society that has left many of us discontent and living lives that are seriously out of balance. In fact, many of us are finding our American Dream has become nightmarish.

The generation of Americans that currently makes up the bulk of our population—the generation that voted our current set of leaders into power—has been insulated and protected from many of the challenges that other people around the world face every day. We have grown up in an era of unimaginable abundance and we've gotten drunk on it. We've forgotten what it takes to really struggle day to day just to put food on the table.

We Westernized citizens spend 80 percent of our time working for profit, thinking that someday we will earn enough money to allow us time to fish and garden. In comparison, the third world citizen spends 80 percent of his time fishing and gardening.

Now we face dramatic changes in our lives and in our expectations, and while many people are ready to embrace the changes, too many people are afraid of releasing the pain they know in order to take a leap of faith into a possible better future. Yet, at the same time we are seeing a surge in spiritual consciousness, which gives me great hope.

Due to an expanding awareness of this insane imbalance of priorities, we are beginning to see growing unrest in the United States and other Westernized countries. In the United States, this unrest will eventually result in upheaval and may lead to the revamping of the U.S. Constitution and the adoption of a global constitution that recognizes the new global citizen and acknowledges that we share one planet.

There was a moment in time in the late 1960s when the U.S. Apollo missions sent spaceships into outer space and sent photographs back to Earth. For the very first time people could see our planet; we saw the whole planet as one world. It was awe inspiring. Breathtaking. For the first time people saw clearly that we are one world, one ocean, one atmosphere. And for a time we acted with a new awareness that every living thing on the earth was connected. We need to get back there.

Citizens of Other Countries Condemn Americans

Citizens in other countries resent Americans because they recognize that the United States is a very small segment of the world's population and yet consumes most of the world's resources. Citizens in other countries hate Americans for their affluence and greed at the expense of everyone else.

They resent people in the United States because we are exporting our culture to other countries and the youth of those countries are embracing our movies, books, and music. They are also adopting the impulsive behavior that is such an integral part of our consumer culture. These nations are seeing their youth fall to the lure of easy drugs, easy sex, and instant gratification. This lifestyle is very attractive to many people, especially those who have never had access to things beyond their most basic and immediate needs.

Like any drug, instant gratification feels good now, but the price is high. As the citizens of many countries see their youth succumb to the Western self-indulgent, decadent lifestyle, as they see their children leave the farms for work in the cities where they have more access to these lures, these citizens are building up a lot of rage and resentment toward Americans.

It is interesting to think that these same countries that are less Westernized and less educated may actually be more resilient in the face of the coming changes than citizens in the United States, Europe, and the other Westernized nations. In many ways their lives will change very little. They will still spend 80 percent of their time gardening and fishing to feed their families. Even the poor in America may see little actual change in their day-to-day activities. They will still be poor. It will be those of us who are deeply invested in the disintegrating American Dream who will see our world turn upside down.

So while less advantaged societies definitely want their standard of living to go up, they may come out of this transformation less traumatized than us Westernized countries. When that occurs, we may begin to see some softening toward Americans for creating such chaos. But even then there are no guarantees, so don't hold your breath.

What Religious Leaders Say about the Pending Economic Meltdown

As always, religious leaders look at the problems around them and use them to support their own beliefs. It doesn't matter what the problems are; religious leaders will find a way to give it spin so they look good. Many have made it their job to stratify and promote differences among people to shore up their power base, and as a result, religious beliefs become more and more polarized, and the distrust among people who think differently spreads like flame.

The truth about religion is that much of religion is based on myth. It's one culture's fantasy versus another culture's fantasy. Every religion believes that they have a monopoly on the truth. Some religions are scarier than others and some are more hypocritical than others, but they all have absolute faith that they have the right to perpetuate their own beliefs.

We must move past that. We must stop letting ourselves be manipulated by political powers, religious powers, talk show hosts, and popular personalities. We must begin to think for ourselves. Honor the truth, and not fantasies. We must stop giving away our power to people just because they say we should.

If being religious means that we blindly follow our leaders, then it is not good for us. If our religion does not promote compassion, it if does not include all life in that compassion, then our religion should be discarded. We should embrace a religion that sanctifies not just human life, but all life as being sacred.

Chapter 4

What People Fear about the New World Order

People fear the unknown. They fear change, especially when that change is out of their control and strips them of power. In the coming economic and social transformation, a lot of control is going to change hands. Politicians, religious leaders, business leaders, and financial leaders all potentially face great loss of power and economic control. They see this coming and fear it.

In an effort to maintain their current power, these powers that be will do their best to distract the people by creating an uncertain environment filled with diversions and distress, so that the people will be too busy trying to navigate the rapid changes and survive day by day and not notice that their leaders are grabbing as much power and control as they can.

These leaders will attempt to terrify people. They will describe a New World Order as a fascist police state where an army of people in uniforms and riot gear, with tear gas, tasers, and armored vehicles will round up citizens and prosecute them for thought crimes. They will describe a world where the few will crush the many with an iron fist. They will describe Italy during World War II. They will do their best to terrify people into continuing to hand over their power and trust to them to do what is best.

And many people will do just that. They will remain in denial amid this distress and they will beg their leaders to save them from this terrible future. This is exactly what the leaders want. They will try to convince their citizens that time will rewind and we can all go back to the way things used to be.

But that is not possible. Too many beliefs have been shattered. Too many mistakes have been made. Too many people realize that too many systems are broken. Too many people are angry and distrustful of their leaders. The time is ripe for upheaval and it cannot be ignored. It's too late.

These leaders will attempt to discredit anyone and anything that threatens their absolute power. Good leaders will be smeared, shamed, or disgraced. Grass roots efforts will be ridiculed, divided, and threatened. The political system will tighten even more and make it more difficult for people to put issues to public vote or add people to the ballots. The media will throw out a lot of red herrings to divert attention away from the power plays going on behind closed doors.

Fear is going to drive a lot of people to doing things they wouldn't normally do. That can't be avoided. Fear is a very powerful emotion and it will attract exactly what people fear. That's why I prefer to focus on the coming changes as opportunities for the world to get into better alignment with itself.

I don't believe we are doomed to an oppressive global fascist state. We are no longer a world of nations isolated from each other. People around the world are no longer isolated and kept ignorant about the way the world works. True, there still are many countries such as North Korea where citizens are oppressed and kept ignorant of anything that might contradict their government's policies and ideologies, but there are many more countries where the people are connected by the Internet and YouTube and cell phones; information seeps into every possible crack like water into dry soil.

I don't believe people truly need be afraid of the future. But I do think people have to be smart and start thinking for themselves. For many populations, especially in Westernized cultures, that will be a major challenge because we've been lulled into complacency and have lost many of our survival skills. We must be willing to step out of our comfort zone and get involved in shaping the changes as they come.

Entropy Is Linear and Irrevocable

Change is always happening and much of it is good. Water evaporates into clouds. Clouds float over land and transform into water that falls on the earth. The earth holds a bunch of little dry seeds that transform into plants at the touch of rain. Change can be a very good thing.

Right now, so many systems on this planet have reached a state of such complexity, they are no longer sustainable. They have become almost paralyzed in their chaos and will soon reach a state where they must change. Some of those systems will reform into more elegant, more sustainable systems. Others will simply collapse and never recover. This is the natural cycle of closed systems and it is called entropy.

In simple terms, entropy is the measurement of the amount of randomness in a closed system. The concept was defined by engineers in thermodynamics as a way to understand how and why the structure of closed systems disintegrate when factors within that system become too complex to be contained within that system.

Entropy is linear. It tends to increase or remain the same; it will not decrease. You can think of it as a kind of clock. Once a system becomes chaotic enough and random enough, it disintegrates and restructures itself in another form. After a certain threshold has been reached, the force of entropy becomes irrevocable. When it finally reaches a flash point, the system disintegrates to be restructured in some other form. To paraphrase Boris Pinsker: You can turn an aquarium into fish soup, but you can never turn the fish soup back into an aquarium.

History is full of examples of how this acceleration of chaos and randomness in closed governmental systems resulted in cultural and political revolutions. Consider the French Revolution of 1789 when the Bastille was stormed and the Royal Family was guillotined; in three years, a monarchy that had ruled for centuries was gone, and old concepts of hierarchy and tradition were replaced with enlightened principles about rights and citizenship. Consider 1773 when a dispute over the right of England to tax the colonies resulted in the destruction of tea in Boston Harbor and begat the fight for independence from British rule and the creation of the United States of America. Consider the Chinese Cultural Revolution in 1966 that resulted in nationwide chaos and economic disarray and years of stagnation.

Entropy is underway globally as government and economic structures grow more random and complex at an increasing rate. Right now, any one of a hundred stress points could trigger a complete breakdown of several closed systems. The recent debt crisis in Greece is such a stress point. So is the immense U.S. deficit, which impacts currency and markets around the globe. Part of the entropy in process right now is the devaluation of the U.S. dollar.

We are watching entropy accelerate in our global economy and it will eventually turn into fish soup. That's what I'm talking about when I talk about the crash of the U.S. dollar. The instability of the current closed global economic system will reach a point where it becomes completely unsustainable and we will see a breakdown of that system. This will trigger the restructuring of a new economic order. This disintegration and restructuring isn't necessarily a bad thing, because, while you can't eat an aquarium, you can eat fish soup.

People Are Fearful When Their Beliefs Are Threatened

Those who weather the coming changes will be those who don't succumb to fear. Much of the anger in the United States is based on fear. Americans are afraid of losing everything they worked for and seeing all their beliefs about how life was supposed to be dissolve along with their wealth. Their fear is justified.

Many of these beliefs about what is right and what is just and what we deserve have been passed down for generations. Some beliefs will help people succeed in the times ahead, but others need to fade away because they no longer have any bearing on our new reality. Beliefs can only be validated and perpetuated if they serve the current moment in time. We need to examine our beliefs and be willing to adapt.

Where do these beliefs come from? We all have inherited some beliefs. We all have adopted beliefs based on our own experience. Along with their physical and mental attributes, parents pass their beliefs down to their children. Parents pass along beliefs they believe will help their child survive, but they can only speak from their own experience about what has worked for them at some specific moment in time.

We need to realize that the game has changed and those old beliefs may no longer be relevant. We need to set our old beliefs aside and assess our new experiences without prejudice, because we have never been here before.

Let me give you an example. A parent tells his child to stay away from the river because he will drown in the river and there are crocodiles in the river. As a result the child never goes near the river. This idea is passed down five generations, but by then the river has dried up, all the crocodiles are gone, and the riverbed is just a dusty canyon. But the warning about the river and the crocodiles has become a tradition in the village and so this descendant child still believes that going to the river is dangerous. Then the village runs out of water. But the warning that had been handed down for generations is too strong and so no one goes to the river. No one finds out that the riverbed is dry, but that there is now a new river on the other side of the riverbed. The belief in the river being dangerous had become so entrenched that no one could overcome it and the village doesn't survive.

This is how cultural traditions evolve. This is why wars can go on for generations. Beliefs are so powerful they can overcome common sense or even survival instincts. Beliefs are so powerful they can trap you and even kill you. At this moment in time, I would wager that nearly the entire population of the world is having some of its most cherished beliefs challenged.

Many people are so deep into their beliefs they refuse to consider other points of view or opinions. They cannot see alternative solutions. Thus, we continue to do the same things we have always done, because it worked in past circumstances. Now when we try those things, we get the same results we got in the past, but we are dealing with entirely different circumstances and those solutions don't work. Yet we are unable to break free of our beliefs and change our behaviors.

Many of our beliefs are not working now, but we are still buying cars we can't afford, homes we can't afford, shelling out $400 for imported alligator handbags and $3,000 for designer suits. We are addicted to our beliefs, and like an addict, we never want to relinquish our addiction; we never want to admit we have an addiction.

Ask most alcoholics. A drinker doesn't want to recognize that they have a drinking problem. They could be drinking every day, having blackouts, and getting sick, but they will continue to deny they are addicted. In this state of denial, the easiest thing for the drinker to do is point the finger at someone else and blame them for the car wrecks, the ruined relationships, and the lost jobs. It is never the drinker's fault.

Many Americans are still in denial about the lost jobs and the changing economy and the global social structure that is evolving so quickly. Many Americans don't want to admit that we are part of the problems plaguing the planet. That's why we point our fingers at our leaders. We are saying the problems are caused by those others, not by us. But we were the ones who voted our leaders into office and put them in power.

Our leaders reflect us, and so when we blame our leaders for their actions, we must also accept responsibility for putting them into office in the first place. They reflect our beliefs. That is why we must be willing to reexamine our beliefs and be willing to adopt new beliefs even when they feel frightening.

Governments Believe They're Too Big to Fail

Now, governments in general and the U.S. government in particular would like us all to believe that they are too big to fail—that their position of power is into perpetuity, that they are invincible and will exist forever. They put up monuments to encourage this illusion of longevity. However, just like the wind and tides, governments come and go. Every government and every empire came into being from some other form of rule. They fought themselves into existence and they can be brought down the same way.

Governments as a whole place great value on their own survival. They've convinced themselves and their citizens that they somehow have the right to rule into perpetuity and they act on that belief. You see this idea in most apocalypse movies. You'll notice that extreme measures are taken to keep the political leaders safe and make sure Air Force One gets off the ground with the First Family on board. This is based on the illusion that the power center must be protected at all costs.

We've seen this illusion played out in history. When the ruling class or family or government entity is threatened, they make every attempt to escape danger so they can return later and assume their positions of power again.

For example, in 1979, after 38 years of rule, Mohammad Rezā Shāh Pahlavi, Shah of Iran, fled the Iranian Revolution with billions of dollars. After the Islamic republic took power, Pahlavi traveled the world, seeking sanctuary and medical care in several countries while the Islamic republic chased after him with extradition papers, determined to drag the Shah back to Iran to stand trial. This ended any illusions Pahlavi had about retaining his power. In 1980, he died in Egypt and is buried in Cairo.

An earlier example comes from the House of Romanov, which was the last imperial dynasty to rule over Russia, reigning for about a century before the February Revolution in 1917 abolished the crown. The Russian emperor Nicholas II and his family fled the country with a fortune in jewels. They were captured and placed under house arrest in the Alexander Palace. On July 16, 1918, the family was told that they would be photographed to prove to the people that they were still alive, so up to that point they still believed they had value to the world and that perhaps they would be returned to power. Instead, Bolshevik authorities entered the room and murdered Nicholas II, his immediate family, and four servants.

The Pahlavi and Romanov families fought for survival even though their reign was over. So, like in those apocalypse movies and those historical examples, we can expect our current crop of leaders to fight for survival and dream about regaining power.

I believe there is a general fear among governments worldwide that we are in a trend toward a global government—toward a New World Order. They fear individual nations will collapse and lose their power.

Many of our current leaders see the writing on the wall. They see that the status quo cannot continue. They see revolt on the horizon and are afraid. Many are scrambling to make escape plans and stuff as much loot as they can in their personal offshore accounts and continue to lie to the people as their own lifeboats depart.

Don't Worry, Be Happy

Each nation has its own version of the same warning: Don't worry, be happy. Their political leaders tell the citizens not to panic; it's all under control. They tell the people to stay calm and that the recession is in recovery and that things are turning around. These leaders seem to think that by saying it, it is so. But it isn't so. No amount of magical verbiage is going to halt or even slow the current momentum toward a complete economic reshuffle on the planet.

Most political leaders don't know what to do about the big problems we face, but they know their citizens expect them to know what to do and to do it. So they do what they do best. They stall. They placate the people with vague speeches, empty promises, and false assurances during carefully staged photo opportunities.

In the United States, some of our more prominent leaders have built entire careers on procrastination and avoidance while smiling for the camera. An event happens in the Gulf of Mexico and they look for good press. They say, "I'm going to make a TV appearance in front of the oil. I'm going to roll my sleeves up and get busy with the problem." They say, "We have a problem with the U.S. dollar and I will have a press conference to talk about forming a committee or describe my three-pronged approach about how I'm going to get busy with financial reform and financial regulation." But their self talk is more along the lines of "I'm going to look really busy while I basically do nothing." And after their press conference, they will call up their cronies for another round of golf.

They will appear on television and squabble among themselves. They will distract us with accusations of bribery and corruption and titillate us with sex scandals. They will point fingers at opposing political factions and provoke the media to make a stink about something somewhere else. Anywhere else. Anything to keep people from looking too hard and too long at the real root causes of our economic dilemma, which is the U.S. government's irresponsible spending of money it does not have and has no hope of getting.

In an effort to look like they are actually doing something, American political leaders will form committees to study the problems and then send those committees away until everyone forgets they exist. Then those committees will accept the appropriate bribes from lobbyists and deliver their reports behind closed doors and then come up with a snappy name for a law they can shove through the House and Senate while they "work out the details."

They tell the people that the government is actively busy doing things to support the dollar and make it strong again. They tell the people that they have a strong dollar policy. But this is not what their actions reveal. Over the last 30 years, the U.S. dollar has lost 97 percent of its value. The truth is the United States wants a weak dollar because it's the only way to get on parity with countries like Vietnam that are taking away U.S. jobs.

Entropy is evident in several systems within the United States. These systems involve the debasement of the U.S. dollar, the poor treatment of our environment, the dependence on fossil fuels, and the tremendous overhanging problem of our out-of-control health care system. These trends are not set to discontinue anytime soon and are obvious to everyone.

China knows it. Bangladesh knows it. Vietnam knows it. Even the man living in the island in the Philippines knows that the United States is not what it used to be. But knowing it doesn't greatly help because we need to be aware that there are few countries that actually have a healthy, functioning economic model. Greece, Spain, Italy, France, Ireland, Britain, Portugal, and the United States of America are all in trouble. Neither communism, capitalism, democracy, libertarianism, nor any hybrid of these systems work. None of these fantasies are functional and so they must be discarded. We need a new form of government that moves past what is no longer working.

The Grab for Dollars from the Taxpayer's Pocket

In response to the collective fear of the American people and the government, the U.S. government has already grabbed $700 billion dollars of taxpayer money for a stimulus package that was supposed to create jobs across the board. The evidence is in. The only sector that saw a significant increase in the number of jobs created has been the government, and many of those jobs were merely temporary census jobs.

To be fair, I went online to www.recovery.gov to see what the government said about how the stimulus money is being spent. First of all, our government spent $10 million on this web site, which is supposed to monitor the funds and make the information available to the public, but I'm not certain the information is all that reliable. And the cost! I had thought that after 2000 and the dot-com meltdown the only people getting that kind of money were the developers of Pets.com.

According to the data shown in Figure 4.1 from this web site, out of the $787 billion the government has collected from taxpayers, approximately $529 billion of it has been spent.

When I looked at the top grant recipients, I found five state governments listed. Obviously, those states were first in line when it came to getting a chunk of taxpayer money. Of course, some big guns in the private sector got loans and contracts.

Digging a little deeper, I went online to check out the United States Department of Agriculture (USDA). I found that some of the stimulus money has provided loans to rural agriculture companies expanding to

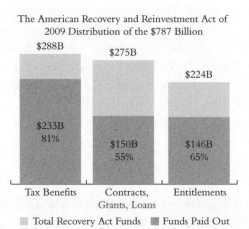

The American Recovery and Reinvestment Act of 2009 Distribution of the $787 Billion

■ Total Recovery Act Funds   ■ Funds Paid Out

Figure 4.1   Stimulus Spending
Source: www.recovery.gov. (U.S. Treasury, federal agency financial and activity reports.) All rights reserved.

keep employees or hire more. One company got $8 million for a giant greenhouse expansion and will hire 43 people, so that's good. And a winery got $3 million to restructure its debt and keep nine jobs. So, basically they avoided bankruptcy. Let's see, that's $11 million dollars for 52 jobs. You do the math.

This still leaves $278 billion dollars unaccounted for on this site. Some of it was bailout money, but shouldn't that be reported, too? Am I alone in wanting to see the books?

If we can't know where all our stimulus money has gone, at least we can get a snapshot of where the United States is in terms of overall debt. Right now the grand total of U.S. debt is around $136 trillion. Here's how it breaks out:

- The official national debt is $13.1 trillion (divided by 300 million U.S. citizens, that's $43,524.05 for each one of us.)
- Unfunded federal obligations of Social Security, Medicare, government pensions, and more equal $107.8 trillion.
- The U.S. federal deficit is $1.6 trillion.
- Another $9 trillion in cumulative deficits is expected over the next 10 years.
- There's $3.5 trillion owed to foreign investors.
- Health care reform is another trillion dollars.

Total: $136 trillion dollars, or $453,000 for each U.S. citizen, man, woman, and child. According to the U.S. Treasury Department, as of May of 2005, official national debt was $7,782,816,546,352. As of January 2008, that figure was $9,193,222,137,000.00 and two years later it has almost doubled at $13,452,058,496,388.20.

But that's not all of it. Again, according to the U.S. Treasury Department, as of May of 2005, our total obligations were $53.6 trillion. In February 2009, the online publication of WorldNetDaily gave that figure as $65.5 trillion, which exceeded the gross domestic product of *the world at that time.* In May 2009, *USA Today* revealed the results of its analysis of overall national obligations and tallied the sum of all U.S. personal and federal government obligations at $63.8 trillion, or $668,621 per American household. And now we sit at $136 trillion, more than double the total five years earlier. Our fear about the unsustainability of this debt crisis is well founded.

A Fearful Government Nationalizes Industries

From banks to automotives to mortgage lending, from health care to college scholarship programs, we are seeing a frightened government grab property and power on a scale that makes the land snatch of America's Western expansion during the 1800s look like an Easter egg hunt.

It's ironic. In the 1920s we were fighting the "Reds." We vilified communism and anything that smelled of government ownership. In the 1950s we watched the McCarthy hearings ruin lives and blacklist hundreds of U.S. citizens on hearsay and sketchy evidence about alleged communist associations. Yet, here we are in 2010 and our administration has alleged ties with subversive groups and aggressively nationalizes entire sectors of our industry.

We have seen the nationalization of the auto industry with the takeover of General Motors and Chrysler. Even though the administration says they are trying to make General Motors (GM) private again, I am not sure how that will play out either short or long term. And to add insult to injury, according to Michelle Malkin in her book *Culture of Corruption,* the current administration decided to shut down Honda dealerships across the country to ensure "equal sacrifice," an act that was arbitrary and deliberately threw thousands more auto workers out of work.

We watched as the government systematically took over sections of the financial industry through Citigroup, Bear Stearns, Washington Mutual, AIG, Fannie Mae, and Freddie Mac, along with a number of other troubled financial institutions. And while they were at it, they took over the student loan programs.

Then national health care legislation was shoved through Congress in a slam-dunk over Easter weekend. This was followed by the Supreme Court opening the doors to unlimited corporate sponsorship of political campaigns and the EPA handing the keys to our water supply to the natural gas companies.

What is going on?!

The government took over these major auto manufacturers because that industry has lots of labor. It has lots of jobs and lots of people making cars that are not economically profitable in the United States. The industry is not viable. It is not profitable because of the unions.

The auto industry pays out tremendous benefits to union members and makes a substandard product. Yet, our administration gave that industry billions of dollars to keep it afloat (because the unions pay for political campaigns and vote in blocks), and now U.S. taxpayers own an industry that is not sustainable.

Why? The government might say it is to preserve jobs, but that's not true. Nothing can save those jobs. Those jobs were going away anyway, because the industry as it exists today is archaic and not competitive. So I think there is something else going on. I believe the administration bailed out the big three U.S. auto manufacturers for three reasons.

One, they did it because of our American pride. They did it to preserve the illusion that the United States of America is still a dominant force in automobile manufacturing. I'm sorry, but that hasn't been true for decades. Two, they caved in to union pressure to preserve their pention funds. And three, I think they did it because the chief executive officers (CEOs) of those companies whined really loud and really long.

None of these reasons makes business sense. But the key members in our current administration in 2010 don't have much experience in the business arena, so they don't understand that a sound business strategy would have been to let the companies go into bankruptcy and use the time to retool and retrain the workforce to manufacture something the planet does want. Then we would have a new industry, new jobs, and new exports.

Now, let's turn to the banking sector. We have a financial industry set up to encourage poor financial management among our citizens while it aggressively promotes no-win investment practices. There's lots of money to be made there so I'm sure there was pressure to keep that industry alive. The financial industry wants to keep consumers spending. It wants consumers to indulge their impulses and rack up more debt by gambling in Las Vegas and Atlantic City, or by buying that car they can't afford.

The government wants the financial sector to be saved so that sector can promote more consumption with credit, which makes the GDP and Consumer Confidence Index look better. The government also wants the financial sector to do well so all those bank CEOs will turn over a big chunk of their bonuses to the political campaign of their choice, just like the U.S. Supreme Court said they could.

Resistance to Change Is the First Response

Americans are justified in our fear that we will lose what we've worked our whole lives to attain. We are justified in our fear that we will be unable to leave our children anything other than debt and a legacy of failure. Already, too many of us have lost our livelihoods, our homes, our retirement accounts, our businesses, and our sense of security. And even while we try to absorb our grief over all our losses, the changes keep coming with increasing speed. Our fear of more change is very understandable.

Our first response to yet more change is resistance. We want to blame someone and make someone else pay for our inconvenience. We've grown used to having what we want when we want it and it's just not fair! We stay stuck in our righteousness and denial and refuse to accept that things have changed forever.

I think part of our resistance is that we are afraid to wake up and give up our treasured beliefs. We are the boy in the bubble, and the bubble just got popped. Our American Dream is dead, and our passivity has become an epidemic that has almost wiped out America.

We don't want to take charge of our own lives, because it's work. We've gotten lazy. We've been brainwashed by the corporations that have trained us that our primary function is to consume. We've been trained that our job is to wake up each day, work at a job we don't like, pay our taxes, and take our measly 15 percent net pay home and spend it on stuff we don't need, watching dated nature shows voyeuristically while the planet's real wealth is in serious peril.

Americans need to gain a new perspective. When we resist and complain about our circumstances, we are forgetting to be grateful for everything we do have. We need to remember that as Americans we still have it easy compared to the rest of the world. We don't have to work in the fields under a hot sun 16 hours a day from dawn to dusk, grow our own food, milk our cow, and beat wheat stalks for grain before collapsing exhausted in bed and having to get up the next day and do it all again. Instead we come home from our air-conditioned office, sip an imported wine, nibble some imported cheese before sinking our teeth into a nice thick Kobe beef steak, and then stimulate our dulled senses with an hour or two of entertainment from among the 1,000,000 television channels we have beamed in from an orbiting satellite, *Wall-e* style.

We must realize that what we resist persists. The more we resist these changes, the more difficult our struggle will be. The more we think about what we've lost, the more we will lose. The more we think about lack, the more lack we have. The more we worry about our family's health, the higher the chances are that one of our kids will get sick or break an arm.

We must realize that we infect the atmosphere with our thoughts. We create exactly what we think about. That may sound like some simplistic, new-thought mumbo-jumbo, but your belief is not required for this to be true. It is a law of the universe and no amount of resistance will change it. It is simply the way it is.

We don't have a road map for how to deal with our current situation, because this generation hasn't faced anything like this before. But our parents did. Our grandparents and generations right back to the inception of this country faced nearly insurmountable obstacles and still managed to create order out of chaos. Now it's our turn.

Chapter 5

How We Can Build and Prepare for the New World Order

The current economic situation in which the world finds itself is already unsustainable. However, people will not really accept that fact until the pain of the situation is greater than the pleasure of believing the fantasy that it might all go back to the way it was. For any of you who have dealt with an addict of any kind, whether they were addicted to alcohol, drugs, sex, or gambling, you know that the only way the person will break their addiction is when there are simply too many wrecks, too many arrests, too many bodies piled up around that person and it stops being fun.

As addicts of fossil fuels, we are starting to see some serious wrecks, crimes, and bodies pile up. We still love the juice of driving our fast cars to the corner convenience store for a loaf of bread, but now we are looking at the environment and it's no fun to see half the Gulf of Mexico under oil. It's no fun to see the wildlife panting as they try to breathe through an inch thick coat of sludge. It's no fun to think that we can't go play on the pretty Florida beaches or eat fresh shrimp from the Gulf without worrying we're swallowing a mouthful of oil. It's no fun to realize our drinking water is full of natural gas. Our addiction to oil has stopped being fun.

Our whole consumer-oriented, live-for-today attitude has led America down a path where we are no longer a going concern. And if our nation is not a going concern, if we are not producing viable, exportable products, then our economy is not sustainable, and our present illusion of comfort is going to disappear. Fact.

But even more damaging to our economy is the fact that our dollar is not sound; it is not based on a metal weight. But it used to be, so let me explain how the Federal Reserve has destroyed our economy.

Who Is in Charge of Our Money?

The Federal Reserve is neither a government entity nor a reserve. It is a private corporation that charges the U.S. government (i.e., the taxpayers) interest on each U.S. dollar it prints. So, instead of the U.S. Treasury being in charge of our currency, we've outsourced that job to the Fed and pay them handsomely for doing the job.

This corporation was set up in 1913 during a committee meeting held at 1:00 A.M. a few days before Christmas. The public was told that it was urgent that the country have a monetary policy independent of the government. (This reminds me a lot of the last-minute Sunday vote to pass Obama's health care bill.)

Of course, the taxpayers were not told the real purpose behind forming the Federal Reserve, which was to make a handsome profit for the shareholders and board members of that corporation at the taxpayer's expense. It was corporate greed right from the beginning even though the name disguised it as a government entity. This led people to believe that the Federal Reserve was controlled by their power as voters. It was a deliberate effort to mislead the American people. Fortunately, we are learning the truth now.

It turns out the so-called independent nature of the Fed has led to increased instability in the country's economy. People have discovered the reality of the U.S. debt; that about 40 percent of the U.S. debt is owed to the Federal Reserve. It's time for the people to end the Federal Reserve's free ride on the taxpayer's dime.

Perhaps the new financial reform bill will do some good, although I don't think it will change the basic function of the Federal Reserve. That is why we need to make plenty of noise and demand major changes in the leadership and organization of that corporation.

- We must stop the money hemorrhaging and the non-stop printing of money.
- We must demand that the power of the Federal Reserve be curtailed and its responsibilities divided up differently.
- We must demand better consumer protection regulations be put into place.
- We must demand an audit of the Federal Reserve.
- Most importantly, we must demand an end to the Federal Reserve's profiteering practices at the expense of every taxpayer in the country.

We simply cannot afford to keep paying this corporation interest on all the money it prints when we don't even want all that money printed! Who asked them to print it? I didn't. Did you? I never saw it put to a vote. No sensible person would have voted for it, because it is against our own interests; the non-stop printing of money dilutes the value of what money you do have, just like when a corporation issues too much stock and dilutes the value of each share.

Rethink the Importance of the Dollar

We need to seriously consider a new currency that is based on real reserves of silver or gold or some other precious commodity. Right now all the central banks around the world are buying gold, including the Federal Reserve. Why do you suppose these central banks are buying gold now when all this time they've been leasing their gold to investment firms? It's because their fiat currencies are unsound.

They are not backed by gold or any tangible asset. Their paper currencies are becoming worthless and they know it.

As individuals, as a Western culture, we need to consider how we really think about the value of the U.S. dollar. We must determine a new set of values based on what is really important, which is clean air to breathe, clean water to drink, clean food to eat. Then we can think about our shelter and how many rooms we want. Then we can think about our cars and how much horsepower we think we need to get where we think we need to go. Really, where do you need to go?

Do a Cost Analysis of Our Diminishing Returns

Look, we're only on this planet for a little while. Things come and things go. Empires rise and empires fall. American politicians rotate every four years. Things can be dreadful today and could be glorious tomorrow. Things change constantly. It is up to people like you and me to make sure those changes are for the better.

Americans live in one of the most free societies on the planet, and we are free to create a new kind of lifestyle. We are a nation of inventors, of get-it-done people. Yes, we've created a lot of dead weight with our entitlements and welfare programs, but brilliance is in our genes and we can think our way out of this mess.

People don't make changes easily. People usually don't make significant changes until they feel enough pain. This enables people and governments to postpone making changes. But we can't really wait until we feel enough pain because by then it will be too late. By then our water will be ruined, our oceans destroyed, our fish gone, and our bodies riddled with diseases caused by the constant consumption of poisons.

That's why we need to do a cost analysis now. We need to do a risk versus reward assessment and decide if our actions have a positive or negative impact on our environment, our economy, and our society.

Many Western societies have been able to postpone making these kinds of difficult choices because they have done one of the following:

- Separated themselves from nature.
- Distanced themselves from the economic consequences of being enabled by debt.

These are two very different things.

Over the past few decades, Westernized society has become more and more separate from nature. We hook ourselves up to our Wii systems, or surf the Net, or chat on Facebook, then watch movies about endangered species and overfishing off the Great Barrier Reef. We don't get out and listen to birds, watch the turtles plop off logs into the water, or feel the brush of a breeze coming off a meadow. We have lost our connection to the environment and replaced it with artificial simulations.

This allows us to remain separate from events that deplete our resources and destroy our habitat. And it is our habitat that is being destroyed, make no mistake. When we hear about "lost habitat," we might think that means South American and Malaysian forests, but habitat is where anything lives. That means us. Our land, our trees, and our water are being destroyed. It's not just the orangutans and dart frogs that are being endangered; it's us! All biological creatures are dependent on nature for their survival. It is in our own selfish interest to look after the environment, and even the Malaysian Tree Frog, because this is where we live. This earth is our home.

My second point is that we continue to distance ourselves from the economic consequences of being enabled by debt. Think about how a store operates. A store can only survive if it has customers and can sell items to generate profits. But now we have stores that run entirely on debt. The store borrows to buy inventory and sells to customers who use credit to buy those goods. It's all paper. No money has actually changed hands. There is no exchange of real value except for the goods, and the consumer has those now.

In this model, the retailer charges what the market will bear and it can bear a lot because the consumer is using credit to buy. That means they can pay what the retailer wants to charge. This drives prices up and up and up until the consumer has maxed out their credit and can't buy anymore. Now the retailer has a store full of overpriced stuff that they paid too much for, and has to sell them at a discount, possibly losing money. You can see how this model has a high potential for *diminishing returns*. A business that continually runs on this model becomes a hollow shell. And so do governments.

Now in 2010, we are at a point where these two factors are converging. As a species we are dependent on all these fragile ecological systems, yet separated from how nature sustains us. We are dependent on our access to credit, yet disconnected from how basic economics function.

Now in 2010, we find that our economy and our environment are intricately intertwined. We cannot continue to live a debt-fueled lifestyle and we cannot continue to deplete the planet's resources. Our Western model of consuming everything in sight for profit and comfort is a lifestyle model with *significantly diminishing returns*.

Let me give you a visceral picture of what this looks like. If you put a frog in a pot of boiling water and you turn up the temperature a degree at a time, then the frog stays comfortable and does not want to get out of the water. The frog is comfortable until the point when the water is hot enough to cook him. Then he starts to scramble to get out, but it's too late. He's half-cooked before he even noticed things had gotten hot. He accommodated the changes degree by degree and never realized he was doomed.

That is what is happening to us. We are boiling in a pot of debt degree by degree. We stay hooked up to our iPods and ignore the fact that the Federal Reserve is printing more and more money every day, charging us more and more interest on those new dollars while our dollar is buying less and less each day.

We are boiling in a pot of pollution and destruction degree by degree and watch stupid television programs while our environment is being raped. At a point in the not-too-distant future, maybe even next month or next year, the temperature in the pot will be high enough to cook us.

We Broke It and We Need to Fix It

Citizens need to band together in various small groups or councils to review the effectiveness of our government entities and the choices they make. We need to get involved and look over the shoulders of our leaders. We need to double-check their books and demand accountability.

We must do the same thing to our own books. We must refuse to allow borrowing from the future to pay for today's wants. We need to tighten our belts, pull up our bootstraps, and stop being wimps.

We need to yank the power from the hands of our incapable leaders and remember that while our forefathers included their share of people escaping prosecution, they also included people escaping persecution. Our forefathers were made up of entrepreneurs, adventurers, and opportunists all seeking the freedom to fulfill their potential. Since then, our nation has welcomed others battered by life and seeking personal freedom. Our forefathers had plenty of grit to start over, and their blood runs in our veins. Can we do less?

The generation currently in power was handed a nation declared a victor in World War II and we have enjoyed a life of almost unlimited bounty. We have depleted that bounty and broken our powerful country. Now it's our job to fix it.

Governments Must Return to What Works

Government and corporations are mostly made of old men in their 60s. The time for them to actually do anything has basically come and gone and they are looking at retirement. Frankly, I believe that many of the people in government are religiously zealous, who believe the economic and environmental apocalypse we are seeing now is the herald for the coming of The Rapture. It's as if they don't care if the whole world goes to hell, because they won't be here. They'll rise into "perfected bodies" in a Celestial Paradise.

I also think that governments in general are unwilling to address the underlying problems of our conjoined and mutually unstable economies and environmental concerns because they fear opening Pandora's box. No one wants to rock the boat and demand some kind of cooperation from the others. So everyone waits. Our leaders will stall as long as possible until the pain becomes unbearable, which means a 19 on a scale of 1 to 10. They will postpone feeling that pain for as long as they can. After all, there is always a good cocktail party waiting, a good golf round to enjoy, and Oprah will be on at 4:00 P.M.

If left to their own devices, our governments will do what they've always done. They will pass the buck and leave the problems for the next guy to solve. They will ignore the country's most pressing problems and adjourn their legislative sessions to campaign for reelection.

I have no confidence that our own current government will do anything except continue to be a giant, all-consuming, parasitic, malignant tumor on society. I expect that trend to continue until citizens become so fed up with the ineptitude of our leaders that we see a social uprising either through the ballots or in the streets—revolt.

Part of preparing for the coming New World Order in the United States is to restructure and rethink the functions of our political system. We can't change how other countries are ruled, but we can change how we rule ourselves. We have to go back to what works, back to the Constitution. We had enlightened people who formed our country and our Constitution. They kept it simple: a government by the people and for the people.

Granted, this was long before we had all our environmental issues and before our society was hooked on trash television and videos, but the basics still apply. Our political system was set in place to serve American citizens and promote noble causes. What we have now is a government that projects itself around the world to defend its economic interests and ignores the interests of its own citizens.

The U.S. government has built itself on the image of the Lone Ranger, forgetting, of course, the contributions of the trustworthy Tonto, who lost his home and family in the westward expansion. (That whole partnership was a beautiful example of Hollywood propaganda, but I doubt many Native Americans appreciated it.) All propaganda aside, today our interest in the world has very little to do with advancing democracy and morality. That hasn't been the case for the last 50 years. We are now a nation that is heavily armed and that projects itself around the world through relationships with large corporations that want to protect their private interests. Our presence on the world stage is mostly an excuse to wage foreign wars for resources, mainly oil.

The Iraq war was over oil. The Kuwait war was over oil. The Vietnam war was over the offshore oil wells around that country. While World War II was raging, the United States stayed out of it until the very end when we rode in to save the day. Yes, we responded to an attack on Pearl Harbor, but if that hadn't happened, it's hard to say just when the United States might have gotten involved.

The bottom line is we got in near the end of that war, and when it came time to sell supplies to a decimated Europe, we were the only

Western economy left standing. That's why from Poland to Fiji they love Spam.

Governments Must Support Innovation, Not Save Dying Industries

Part of our preparations for the changes is to rewrite government's job description so that its priority becomes the support of free enterprise, rather than the over-regulation and taxation of entrepreneurs. We need to remove the stranglehold on businesses and set them free to do what Americans do best: Innovate and find solutions.

The government has tried to slow or stop the coming changes by clamping down and grabbing control of some of the major industries in this nation. This is a waste of time, energy, and money and only delays the inevitable. History shows us that the free enterprise machine can make this country prosper.

We need to let the free markets determine who survives and who fails. We need to let some of those big firms fail. Let them declare bankruptcy. It is not uncommon for companies to continue conducting business even while restructuring due to bankruptcy. These major industries should be allowed to go through the normal business cycle. They can keep producing whatever it is they produce while their financial underpinnings are adjusted, while they rescale their workforce and retool their production lines. If it is a viable industry, then it will survive. If it isn't viable, it should be allowed to fail.

The U.S. government needs to stop repaying past favors with cash infusions and start encouraging technology and innovations that big business has crushed in the past. Good ideas have been shelved because they threatened the existing energy producers. We will likely see some of these technologies resurface and we need to assess them for their worth. It is even possible we will see low-cost or free technologies made available that will allow households and communities to generate their own energy. This will release more people from the existing power grids that generate energy by burning fossil fuels. We need to create demand for alternative energy sources and demand that government programs encourage development of these sources.

We must encourage our governments to create tax-free, entrepreneurial zones in cities such as Detroit where manufacturing has died out. For example, start-up businesses in these zones could pay no tax on their income and capital gains for some fixed period, maybe 20 years. Such tax empowerment zones could provide incentive and the grace period necessary for new industries to become established in these labor-rich areas. This kind of tax holiday could create a lot of activity and creativity.

Vote on Character, Not by Party

In the United States we are starting to see a voting trend that I think is hopeful. More and more people are voting on character and on track records. People are becoming much more cynical about our leaders and realize every party has its share of unscrupulous people. As a result, fewer voters are willing to just push the blue button or the red button. There are times when I don't want to push either button. I just listen to who is talking common sense and who is talking nonsense.

Right now much of the Democratic Party has moved from left of center to left of left and then extreme left. The Republican Party has also seen a shift. Yes, there are still extreme right-wing conservatives, but much of the Republican Party is now right of center and center. The truth is that more and more people are simply abandoning party lines because they don't mean anything. This is good. We must not allow ourselves to be lulled into the game that pits Republicans versus Democrats. It's a mindless, endless game, a circular tape loop that goes nowhere. It only serves the members of each party.

We are seeing more people declare their independence from the two parties. More people are willing to jump parties and vote for individuals rather than straight party tickets. This means that voters face more challenges when it comes to figuring out who will do a good job in office. We get distorted news about both parties and about individual politicians. It is difficult to know what is true and what is not, so it is especially important that voters do their own research and vote for people based on the content of their character and their track record and not just their political affiliation.

Party affiliation is one of those beliefs that no longer serves any real purpose. It is just another fantasy promoted by a government dedicated to its own survival at any cost.

And while we are abandoning this outdated belief, we need to stop blaming the government for all our ills and stop expecting government to solve all our ills. We need to start downsizing the government and supporting quality candidates who represent the interests of the people who put them into office.

We Need to Learn to Feed Ourselves

Short term, we need to prepare ourselves for the potential chaos that will unfold when people start feeling the impacts of their dependent lifestyles drying up. That means creating a supply of staples. Short term we need to find ways to supplement our food sources. Long term we need to break our dependence on others to supply our food.

Unfortunately, we have forgotten the basics on how to feed or farm for ourselves. We don't know how to grow orchards. We don't know how to can beans or make preserves or pack potatoes or salt meat for winter storage. Most of us don't have any kind of relationship with our food at all. We don't think about where it came from. We don't give a thought about the person who grew it and harvested it. Or the slaughterhouse that cut it up into handy packages that let us forget we're eating another living creature.

We are very detached from the food we put in our body. When we want an apricot, we go to the grocery store, peruse the produce section, and maybe get a little irked when we can't find fresh apricots, but decide to settle for canned fruit. But we are still buying a product.

Now, imagine walking outside in an apricot orchard one morning when the air is still cool. The trees stand in endless rows, their green leaves rustling in the wind. You see hundreds of golden globes nestled among the leaves and smell the rich sweetness of rotting fruit on the ground. Yellow jackets devour fallen fruit on the ground and a stray cat might be snoozing in the shade under a tree. Now you spy the apricot of your dreams and reach up, grasp the soft fuzzy fruit, and give it a little tug to pull it from the branch. You rub your fingers over the fuzzy skin and bring it to your nose to smell that unique apricot smell. You bite through the skin and taste the juice as it bursts over your tongue. You savor the flavor as you chew and smile, knowing you will recall the memory. Then you gather a few more apricots to share with your family.

That is having a personal relationship with the food that goes into your body. But that is not what we have now. Instead, we have this lifeless, cold-packed, plastic-wrapped six-pack package of apricots that has lost 80 percent of its flavor and nutritional value traveling in chemicalized cold storage from the Midwest to the East Coast. We are totally disconnected from our food and this is just unhealthy.

We Need to Reduce Our Sprawl

Did you know that 75 percent of the earth's land mass has been affected by human activity? Our sprawl is like a parasitic growth on the surface of the planet. We need to start building vertically instead of horizontally and leave more land to grow food. We need to create more centralized living, which is much more efficient in the long run.

Centralized living allows communities to literally share common ground. Communities can plant gardens on roofs and the sides of tall buildings, on the plots of land between buildings. They can share common utility lines and recreation facilities. We are already doing this, but we can do more.

In the United States we have plowed under much of the farmland surrounding our cities. We build subdivisions of houses on this rich earth and give them names like Eagle Glen and Bella Vista. We plant lawns instead of gardens and cover them with fertilizers that run into our water systems. We pour concrete for roads that keeps water from sinking into the earth to replenish our water table. And we repeat this all over the United States. It's a tragedy. We must stop this. We cannot continue to plow under our farmland.

The good news is that there are people in some cities such as Detroit who are reclaiming some of this suburban sprawl and restoring it to farmland. They are proof that we can stop this destruction of our farmland and return to what works.

Where Are the Bees?

I'm not just talking about the land. Did you know that in Japan there is a valley that has no bees? They grow pears there. And for the past dozen years they have had no bees to pollinate the trees. They killed all their bees with pesticides, and we are doing the same thing in the United States. We have to import bees now, because our own bees are so clogged up with pesticides that they can't fly. They can't work. They can't make honey. They can't pollinate our trees. Instead, they are dying in astonishing numbers.

In that Japanese valley, the people climb the trees and walk out on the branches of huge pear trees and use special little feather-tipped wands to pollinate the pear blossoms. Everyone does this—the men, women, and kids do this. Sometimes they fall and break their arms. But if the community wants pears to eat and export, they have to climb thousands of trees and do "bee duty," dusting pollen from one blossom to the next. That's insane and we are heading in the same direction. We need to stop stuffing our bees with poison.

We need to grow a generation of farmers, people who will work the land and grow produce to feed the world. Support these local growers by buying from the farmers' markets that are springing up all over. You can buy cheese, milk, yogurt, and all kinds of produce that is made locally. You can raise chickens and eat fresh eggs. You can reduce your consumption of meat and eat more grains and legumes. These are lifestyle changes that can have a profound impact on our own lives and on the lives of our children. I guarantee you'll be healthier, too. And the day after the dollar crashes, you'll need this, so start now!

We Can Move Mountains

The other thing we need is faith. We need faith in each other, in ourselves, and in our country. I'm not pushing any particular religion, but I believe that faith is a common tenet in all religions.

It is said that faith can move mountains. It is the single element that is constant in the stories of survivors of horrific events. The spiritual faith that our founders relied on fortified their commitment to making this country great and gave them the courage to take huge risks. On faith, they rejected the rule of the most powerful nation in the world at that time and fought unwaveringly until they had moved that mountain. The soldiers and citizens who shaped this nation made great sacrifices yet kept faith in the rightness of their commitment.

If you've studied the masters, you know that faith does have incredible power. Jesus, Buddha, and Allah taught ideas that transformed the hearts and minds of millions of people around the planet. The ideas of Martin Luther King and John Fitzgerald Kennedy transformed our own country.

Americans are creative, courageous, and compassionate. We need to take action, share our ideas, and act with faith in our God, in our nation, in ourselves, and in our own hearts.

So, be in conversation with family, with friends, and with your communities. Participate in public forums and start talking about transformative change. Let your voice be heard in the current void of common sense.

Your Conscious Shift to Oneness

Let me tell you a true story about the Hundredth Monkey. In Japan, there is an island that is inhabited by monkeys. Troops of this particular species of monkey lived in the wild, too, but the island troop was isolated from any wild monkeys. Over time scientists observed that this isolated troop had developed some skills that were unique from the skills used by the wild monkeys. They focused on a particular set of skills and watched as one by one the monkeys in the isolated troop adopted this new behavior. Eventually, the entire troop of about 100 monkeys was doing it.

At about the same time, scientists observing the wild troops noticed this same new behavior showing up in their troop of monkeys. This behavior had never been documented before and the wild troops had no contact with the island community. Yet, somehow, the skill that the island monkeys had mastered was transmitted to monkeys hundreds of miles away. It was as if they shared one big monkey mind.

There was more to the experiment, but some of the scientists started thinking about what had happened and came up with a theory that there was some sort of unconscious link, some tipping point where unique knowledge became universal knowledge and these monkeys were tapped into it.

Regardless of your belief or disbelief in that idea, it is still true that the actions of one person can trigger massive change. Just ask Rosa Parks. When she refused to give up her seat on that bus in 1955, she triggered a bus boycott by the black community in Montgomery, Alabama. It took a year, but those buses were desegregated.

So, don't think that you are powerless. The moment you change your mind or your behavior, you might become that hundredth monkey that tips the scales on this planet by adding your mental energy to some master mind we all share. One person can make a difference simply by taking some action. That action sets up an intention and that intention changes the energy on the planet. That might be a new idea for some of you, but the good news is you don't have to understand how it works, or even believe that it works. Your belief is not required. Just try it.

We Are a Global Village

My wife and I had our first child on the island of Saint Thomas in the Caribbean. We moved down there as an escape from New York City. I did not want to have my child born in Manhattan. I knew that would not be healthy for her. I had been in my career for a number of years. I made a lot of money in the 1990s and we moved down to a tiny island mostly composed of the national park with a population of 3,000 people. It was a small community and you could not escape your neighbors. Everyone knew each other and each other's business. It was the type of community where you had to wave to people. You had to wave; it was expected. And you had to treat the West Indian ladies with respect. You had to greet them with "Good morning, Ma'am" and "Good

(continued)

We Are a Global Village (continued)

afternoon, Ma'am." And if you didn't, you were being uncouth and the ladies would let you know about it.

Over the years, we had three children in the Caribbean. And our friends had children, too. Once we had a birthday party with no fewer than 120 kids running around and making noise. It was glorious. It was a celebration of the whole island. It was all on the beach and it was a beautiful, wonderful day. Here's what I felt. I felt that my children were my neighbor's children. And I felt that my neighbor's children were my children. And I loved my neighbor's child as much as I loved my child. And I felt a sense of responsibility toward the other children, in fact, as much as I did toward my own child. I came away from that day knowing that my child is your child and your child is my child.

We could transition on a global basis to view things that way. Whether it's the premier of North Korea, the head of Iran, China, or Mexico, we would recognize that my child was as important as their children. We would continue to bicker as adults, but as parents, what are we leaving to our children?

Think Globally and Act Locally

As citizens of this world it is immoral for us to pass the problems we've created on to future generations. It is imperative that each one of us take some stand, take some action to reclaim America and this earth. Economically, ethically, morally, and spiritually, this nation is at a crossroads. The decisions we make in the next days, months, and years will leave a legacy for generations to come.

- Take a stand.

    We can participate in established movements to protect our oceans and wildlife or form our own advocacy groups that demand that mega-farmers stop putting poisons and chemicals on our food. Or we can take on the FDA to ban hormones in our food chain and BPA in our plastics and to reclassify naturopathic remedies so that they can be administered by doctors.

- Pick your passion.

    We can become active in curtailing the destruction of our precious farmland. We can buy local produce and support local organic farms. We can block the development of more housing subdivisions and more concrete. We can volunteer to preserve and protect our city parks and green spaces. We can volunteer at the local animal shelter and find homes for abandoned animals. With so many places needing our energy and intelligence, we really have no excuse for sitting on the sidelines. And if you think you can't find the time, then look into the eyes of your child and explain it to them.

- Be kind.

    We can be kind to every person we meet, from the letter carrier to the baker, the firefighter to your neighborhood police officer. Be kind. Follow Gandhi, Christ, Buddha, and Allah. Think about your impact on the world. Thoughts are things. Changing the world starts with changing of our minds. The world is the sum total of our collective thoughts.

- Buy what has already been made.

    Do you really need to buy something new all the time? When you buy something that has already been manufactured, you are not using up more resources from the environment. Maybe you can buy a used car instead of a new one. There are good social companies like Goodwill, Salvation Army, and St. Vincent DePaul that sell secondhand goods that are just fine.

    Rather than clearing a lot and cutting down trees, consider buying one of the millions of houses that are already standing. It's true that the mad real estate rush caused a lot of crap to be built, but some of the older houses used good solid wood and not walls made of sawdust and plasterboard. By buying what already exists, you preserve resources and help your pocketbook at the same time.

- Share your hope.

    Speak up when you see something that doesn't make sense. Sometimes all a person needs is a word, a phrase, a sentence, a seed, a spark, an idea that will grow inside them. Be the person who spreads light, possibility, and hope. Not just to your family, although that is the first place to start. Do it now.

Be a Leader and Turn the Herd

I remember when I was a boy sitting on the porch at my Grannie's camp on George's Pond in Maine. We were watching the water and it was one of those peaceful moments I return to with great fondness. As the sun set, the fireflies started to come out and my Grannie and I watched as first one lit up, then another, then another until there were dozens, then hundreds of little lights flying around in the night. It was an amazing sight and I remember wondering, as only a young child can wonder, how they all knew when to turn their lights on. It was like they were all connected by some invisible cosmic web.

But what made the first one light up? That's what we need to ask ourselves now. What makes the first firefly light up and start the change that then lights up the night? What will make the first person light up and become visible and be an example for others. We need to be willing to think, plan, and act differently. We need to be willing to take some risks. We need to be willing to leave our comfort zone, to step into a bit of discomfort and make a difference.

I'm stepping out and becoming visible by writing this book. And every night, before I go to bed I say a prayer. Every night that prayer is a prayer of love for my family, for my neighbors, for my community, for my country, and for the world. Consider doing likewise. As we change ourselves, the world will change with us.

Take It to the Street

It is difficult to talk about these overwhelming, grandiose problems without feeling helpless. We think "I'm just one person and I can't change the world and since I can't change the world, I won't change anything. I'm comfortable doing things a certain way, so I'm going to keep doing that."

As Americans we must lead the charge to introduce innovations and solutions to meet the inevitable challenges of new kinds of economic forces. We can begin by changing our own expectations and taking personal action to get ourselves in alignment with reality.

Global change is already underway. Already millions of people have changed their habits either voluntarily or due to duress. The truth is that individuals like you and me are already transforming our world by changing our minds and our hearts. As we transform individually, we transform the world with us.

This is where you start preparing for the New World Order. You can become an agent for global transformation by changing your own thinking first, following what your heart tells you to do, and doing what needs to be done.

- We need to remember that we are biological creatures and we need basic things like a healthy habitat and healthy food.
- We need to stop poisoning our own environment by recycling our oil, old prescriptions, and household toxins property and stop dumping them in the ditch, in the toilet, or down the drain.
- We need to stop financially supporting corporations that abuse the environment by boycotting their products.
- We need to become active members of the human species instead of passive citizens of particular countries. I don't want to wrap myself up in the U.S. flag any more than I want to wrap myself up in the European flag, or the Chinese flag. The flag I want to wrap myself up with is the flag that says that I am a part of this planet. Our allegiance needs to be to every living thing in this world—every human being, every whale, every dolphin, every bird, every snake, and every insect. Our allegiance needs to be to all life, because all life is precious.
- We need to reach out to others and start creating synergy about the changes we want to see in our governments and in our businesses.
- Businesses owners need to resurrect promising technologies and find new applications for old technologies.
- We need to become activists. Demanding changes and account-ability requires a coordinated grassroots effort.

Here's the truth. Change is inevitable and it is constant. Today's lake bed is tomorrow's sedimentary rock. Today's tide is tomorrow's rain. Survival requires that we adapt to the changes that are underway. We must commit to becoming the change we want to see in the world.

Chapter 6

What to Expect the Day the Dollar Crashes . . . and Beyond

U p to this point I've talked mostly about the unsustainability and the global abuse of our planet and of the unsustainable U.S. national debt and the unsound U.S. dollar. But many other countries also carry unsustainable debt and their currencies are unsound as well. It is inevitable that we will reach a point where all this instability and unsustainability reaches a breaking point.

What would that look like?

- Would the U.S. dollar crash and become worthless?
- How might the crash of the U.S. dollar happen?
- What would the world powers do in response?
- What could investors do?
- What would happen socially in the aftermath of such a crisis?

So many questions and here I am without my crystal ball. Fortunately, I have insight instead and a lot of business sense.

A Country Is Like a Business

I compared currencies to common stock earlier on, so let's stick with that idea. We'll think of global currencies as shares of common stock in each relative nation.

Now, when a company becomes insolvent, it can declare bankruptcy, sell off all its assets, apologize to its shareholders, and conceivably the executives can walk away with a blot on their credit report and start over.

It's not quite that simple when we're talking about currencies and countries. Companies typically operate independently. One company could fail and several other companies in that sector might also take a hit, but they wouldn't necessarily fail. However, the economies of our world's nations are deeply intertwined, which means what happens to one will have a major impact on the others.

Right now the U.S. economy is funded by debt and so are the economies of countries in Westernized Europe. That makes them and us insolvent and vulnerable. If at some point the currency in one of those countries loses significant value on the exchange markets, some predictable things could happen.

I suppose it could start with instability in a European country such as Greece or Spain, but that already happened, and while we certainly saw some instability, the other member nations of the International Monetary Fund (IMF) came to the rescue and, for the moment, prevented a full-scale global meltdown. But for this model, since the United States is the major debtor nation on the planet, I'm going to assume that when this really big trigger is pulled, it will take everyone down with it.

Here's the short version.

Some debt-related crisis triggers a lack of liquidity and a rise in interest rates. We quickly see a conflagration of interactions as international markets manipulate interest rates to attract bond and note buyers. Instability increases and we see a stampede to buy currencies of countries with hard assets and resources. This is followed by a global meltdown of all stock markets. Markets seize up. Some entity, possibly the IMF, might step in and attempt to stabilize the currency market, which might require resetting the debts of all nations and issuing a new currency to keep markets open.

Okay. Now let's take it a little slower.

The Day the U.S. Dollar Crashes

To give you an idea of how the collapse of the U.S. dollar might occur, I've prepared a possible time line for how this might unfold.

10:00 A.M. EST Wednesday. The U.S. government is having its regular auction of U.S. Treasury notes. Here we go again begging to the world with our tin cup. Only this time the world says, "No. We aren't going to buy any more U.S. IOUs." This would be a real shock to the global markets and things could get dicey, but no one is willing to make the big move to send everything crashing down because they might be wrong and the IMF or someone might step in and buy those bonds. Then, over the weekend, because of the global instability, we could expect some kind of announcement about the situation. It won't be comforting.

3:00 P.M. EST Sunday. When the Asian markets open, we see a meltdown. The Asian markets are down 5 percent, then 6 percent, then 7 percent in an all-out free fall. It touches off an avalanche of selling and markets around the world go into independent free falls.

3:00 P.M. EST Sunday. Global currencies start to slip and are also in free fall. Gold prices rise by $300 to $400 dollars an ounce. Silver and palladium are also up as global investors convert, to put everything they have into precious metals.

9:30 A.M. EST Monday. The New York Stock Exchange (NYSE) opens and within minutes circuit breakers around the world pop under a deluge of market orders.

9:50 A.M. EST Monday. The NYSE is advised of the problems of liquidity and the market shuts down. Markets around the world react with volatility in a strong down trend. All the nations need liquidity, but all of the treasure that the United States and Western Europe had has been shipped to China and the Middle East. No one else has any liquidity. We start to witness competition for the remaining global liquidity. Everyone starts selling bonds to raise capital, but there are few buyers. Prices plunge; yields rise.

10:10 A.M. EST Monday. Markets around the world react to the close of the NYSE with volatility in a strong down trend.

10:45 A.M. EST Monday. Several countries in Europe announce they have raised interest rates by 3 or 4 percent to make their own bonds attractive to buyers. In response, other global markets become very nervous and even less stable.

9:30 A.M.   EST Tuesday. The NYSE is unable to open due to the quantity of sell orders jamming the systems.

9:45 A.M.   EST Tuesday. The Federal Reserve calls an emergency meeting. The United States needs liquidity and must compete for it.

10:45 A.M. EST Tuesday. The Federal Reserve announces a hike in interest rates.

11:15 A.M. EST Tuesday. Global markets don't the hike in U.S. interest rates but respond by seeking some type of footing for the short term.

11:30 A.M. EST Tuesday. The NYSE finally manages to open two hours after the opening bell. Global markets have gapped down 6 to 7 percent from Friday's close.

12:05 P.M. EST Tuesday. Traders believe the worst is behind them.

Tuesday afternoon through Friday morning. The dollar rallies. Markets find new levels. Traders around the world are walking on eggshells and having a hard time sleeping. Global currencies are still in free fall. Gold prices continue to rise along with other precious metals as more buyers come in.

2:00 P.M.   EST Friday. In spite of the hike in interest rates, the U.S. dollar continues to fall as global confidence continues to erode.

8:00 A.M.   EST Saturday. The Fed reconvenes.

10:00 A.M. EST Saturday. Members of the Fed contact their insiders, the White House, and other power brokers and give them a heads-up.

3:00 P.M. EST Sunday. The Fed announces second interest rate hike in as many weeks. At Asian open, China gets first crack at the higher yield bonds.

3:01 P.M. EST Sunday. Currency markets instantly respond as bank interest rates in Western Europe are hiked simultaneously with the United States, but there are no buyers.

9:30 A.M. EST Monday. At the NYSE bell, all hell is unleashed. Traders around the world become net sellers of equities, bonds, and Western currencies. Everyone wants out at the same time. The world markets are thrown into chaos. Panic and confusion sweep the globe and all markets are in free fall.

9:42 A.M. EST Monday. Everything is jammed as the volume of selling off all distributed equities in all the global markets becomes overwhelming. The markets around the world seize up. Trading ceases.

9:45 A.M. EST Monday. The NYSE floor. You can hear a pin drop.

9:48 A.M. EST Monday. The NYSE floor. Someone whispers, "Is it over?" No one responds.

9:50 A.M. EST Monday. The NYSE floor. Someone calls 911 for an aid car. Someone had a heart attack. Make that four aid cars. A woman walking her Chow on the sidewalk outside the NYSE is struck by the falling body of 53-year-old senior stock broker at an NYSE member firm. Pedestrians dodge falling bodies. 911 is swamped with emergency calls.

10:06 A.M. EST Monday. New York. Sirens scream as multiple police cars, ambulances, and medic vans weave through traffic and arrive at the intersection of Broad and Wall Streets. Police cordon off surrounding blocks and clear the area of spectators. New York's finest swarm the NYSE and prevent four suicides.

10:11 A.M. EST Monday. On the NYSE floor. Someone turns up the volume on CNN and people slowly gather around the screen to watch videos of bodies falling out of exchange headquarters in Tokyo, Singapore, Hong Kong, London, Frankfurt, Paris, and Bucharest. Someone turns off the sound, but the videos keep playing.

10:28 A.M. EST Monday. The NYSE floor. Traders start to pick up their tickets. Every hand is shaking. Throughout the day, shocked traders wander out of the building. Some find their way home. Others are never heard from again. Others begin to obsess about how to recoup their losses if and when the market reopens.

10:30 A.M. EST Monday. The Oval Office. The red phone starts ringing. No one answers the phone. The President is on the golf course.

12:01 A.M. EST Tuesday. The IMF convenes with G20 leaders to discuss a solution to the paralyzed markets. They realize the only way to unfreeze the markets is to do a total restructure of all Westernized debt in one fell swoop. This will require a complete realignment of currencies as it will likely include massive workouts by debtor nations. The workouts will mandate that all countries submit to terms set out by a new global authority that is quickly being formed. A fly on the wall hears it all and drops dead.

6:00 A.M. EST Tuesday. A spokeswoman for the IMF/G20 coalition holds a news conference before the New York Stock Exchange opens. The conference is simulcast around the world in multiple languages. She assures viewers that everything is under control and that the IMF/G20 coalition will be overseeing an economic reset that will transpire in an orderly manner. She encourages people to remain calm, that while the temporary halt in exchange trading is awkward, everybody's money is safe and there is no need to panic.

6:01 A.M. EST Tuesday. People panic.

6:45 A.M. EST Tuesday. Police and militia around the world go on alert.

1:58 P.M. EST Tuesday. Every ATM in the United States has been depleted.

2:00 P.M. EST Tuesday. New York. The first bank window is broken. The first bullet is fired. Gun shops are looted. Fighting breaks out for every possible reason.

2:08 P.M. EST Tuesday. Chicago. The first bank window is broken. The first bullet is fired. Gun shops are looted. Fighting breaks out.

2:20 P.M. EST Tuesday. Los Angeles. The first bank window is broken. The first bullet is fired. Gun shops are looted. Fighting breaks out.

3:15 P.M. EST Tuesday. Around the country. Panic spreads. Bank runs are reported. Looting spreads from banks and gun shops to grocery stores and supply stores. Riot squads are deployed. The National Guard is called in. Police start recording fatalities. People start firing back at the police.

4:00 P.M. EST Tuesday. The President makes a nationally televised announcement calling for calm. A 38-year-old unemployed construction worker puts a brick through the Oval Office window and is shot dead by the Secret Service.

4:10 P.M. EST Tuesday. The President and the First Family move to the safe room. *Air Force One* is scrambled.

4:37 P.M. EST Tuesday. The President and First Family are removed to an undisclosed location.

5:00 P.M. EST Tuesday. News of the White House shooting hits the news wire. Police around the country deploy crowd control forces including equine and canine divisions.

Throughout the night video news crews send images to their stations. In major American cities, terrified viewers lock their doors, load their shotguns, hide their children, and watch images of the mayhem on their televisions with the sound off so they can hear if the yelling outside is coming closer.

Near dawn the images on American television begin to include images of street violence in other parts of the world. Militia are prominent.

6:00 A.M. EST Wednesday. A spokeswoman for the IMF/G20 coalition holds a news conference that is simulcast around the world in multiple languages. She implores people to remain calm. She announces a web site URL for people to log on to for updates about the discussions being held to work out the global economic crisis.

6:02 A.M. EST Wednesday. The server for the IMF/G20 web site crashes due to overload.

Hourly updates are broadcast from the White House. The President holds a daily live news conference for selected media representatives but takes no questions.

Nine days after the Great Global Freeze: In the United States, the tally of citizens dead in street riots stands at 3,278, including 212 police officers and government workers. Also, 22 horses and 13 dogs are dead. Arrests of looters stands at 15,012. Arrests for general mayhem stands at 45,356. Bank runs and looting destroyed 279 banks; 32 bank employees were killed, 308 were injured.

6:09 A.M. EST Tuesday. The IMF/G20 coalition holds a news conference that is simultaneously webcast in multiple languages. As a panel, the IMF/G20 coalition members outline the plan to restructure the global economy. They announce the establishment of a new Global Unification Exchange System (GUES) and mandate that all nations cease printing national currencies. They announce that nations participating in GUES need to submit formal reports of their current economic status to serve as a benchmark for the restructuring of debt and reallocation of global credit through GUES. The panel outlines the mandates GUES will follow during the restructuring process and announces a schedule of meetings addressing aspects of the new economic order and provides web sites where people can read the proposals and submit comments. It's a global town hall.

11:10 A.M. EST Wednesday. The newly formed grassroots Coalition for Political Reform/USA (CPR/USA) launches a coordinated Internet campaign to demand changes in the American political system, specifically the elimination of the Electoral College and the creation of a secure online voting system that will ensure one person, one vote and be run by volunteers across the nation.

Pretty scary stuff. Obviously, this is all conjecture. Still, it contains some possibilities that need to be considered as the U.S. dollar continues to weaken. Now, let's focus a bit longer on the restructuring process.

New Game, New Rules

The rule of the market is this: He who has the treasure makes the rules.

The United States doesn't have the treasure anymore, but we do have the weapons, so our strength gets us a seat at the bargaining table.

China, the Middle East, and some other countries hold the treasure, but this doesn't guarantee them complete control. They are just holding the purse strings at this point and we won't see an immediate expansion of their global influence and power.

The problem for Westernized economies is one of ego. The Westernized economies, including the United States, have held the economic lead for a long time, but now they have become beggar nations and can no longer dictate terms for the world.

We are at a point where the whole economic system is broken down. This is the result of the entropy I talked about earlier. The only way for the whole thing to balance itself out is for a global reset. This is sort of like a bankruptcy or a renegotiation of a debt. Let me give you an example. A poor man is leveraged up to his eyeballs in debt and as a result he declares bankruptcy. His debt is reduced or removed and that man now becomes a great person to lend to again. He is given credit again. How can that be? Hasn't the guy just proved he's a bad risk?

Yes and no. To understand how this works, we need to back up a little and understand where bankruptcy laws came from and how they've changed. The first bankruptcy laws appeared in 1592 in England and were designed to benefit creditors, who would file against a company unable to pay its debts and then seize all of the company's assets in compensation. Then the debtor was thrown in jail; they were considered criminals because they didn't pay their debt.

Nowadays, bankruptcy laws allow debtors to file insolvency instead of waiting for the creditor to file against them. This allows the debtor to make a preemptive strike as it were, by petitioning the courts to let them reduce, restructure, or eliminate their debt. In some cases, company and personal assets might be liquidated to pay creditors, but other times the debtor can walk away practically debt free. That's because the focus now is more on debt restructuring, which allows a business to reduce its debt in a number of ways, including paying only a portion of or none of the debt owed. This means the creditors take the hit, not the debtor.

In today's world, the debtor isn't considered a criminal for not paying his debts. Instead, with debt-restructuring he can even continue to run his now liability-free company. Then when it becomes a good candidate for credit again, they get to borrow more money.

When you apply the bankruptcy debt-restructuring procedure to nations, the amount of sovereign debt that would have to be written off is staggering. But all the sovereign debt we hear so much about is pretty much worthless because it is debt that no one can repay. It's called sovereign debt because it is debt owed by a sovereign nation, but it's just a noble sounding name for government debt, also known as public debt or national debt.

This debt can be external debt, which is money or credit currently owed to another nation along with the future interest due on the borrowed funds. Sovereign debt can also include internal debt, which is current and future debt a nation owes to its own taxpayers through pensions and entitlements. So you see, the sovereign debt of any one nation can be a really big number.

Now, governments usually borrow this money or credit by issuing securities, government bonds, and bills that come due within varying time frames. Short-term debt is typically due within one year, medium-term debt is due between 1 and 10 years, and long-term debt is due after 10 years. Less creditworthy countries sometimes borrow directly from supranational institutions such as the European Union (EU), which is an economic and political group composed of 27 member states located primarily in Europe.

But I'm getting away from my point. My point is that when we have a collapse of the economic system, all this debt will need to be eliminated, because there isn't enough liquidity anywhere to actually pay it all off. Some of this debt might be written off and simply go away and the nations that loaned the money by buying our bonds will be out of luck. It's possible some effort might be made to restructure some of the debt, but this would only delay the inevitable.

When this reset occurs, all the sovereign debt in the world will be worth less than toilet paper—picture Enron stock. At least toilet paper has some practical purpose. Once all this sovereign debt is eliminated, the world can start over again with a new currency or some standard form of global exchange.

What will follow will be the formation of a new form of global exchange that will allow countries and individuals to conduct trade and keep the world's economies, institutions, and governments functioning. What we will see will be a realignment of global governments and the creation of a new form of currency to replace all global currencies. This will become the default Coin of the Realm. It will be the new reserve currency.

This might be based on some tangible resource such as gold, silver, palladium, or some other metal. Or it might entail some kind of debit/credit system that eliminates the need for folding money or actual coinage. I don't have a crystal ball so I can't say. But I can say that however the value of this new form of exchange is determined, it will need to be equitable and will no doubt involve some very tense negotiations.

This is the beginning of the New World Economic Order. It will come about from a worldwide economic collapse. Governments will be relatively civil in their efforts to restore order. It is unlikely that any of the major world leaders would be ignorant enough to try to take control by force, because it wouldn't give them what they want, which is economic power.

However, some leaders of smaller countries are that ignorant and may make desperate attempts to grab power through force, so we may see some civil bloodshed due to emotions and panic running high. But this is an economic watershed and the focus of the world will be on restoring economic order, so it is unlikely that the leaders working to establish this order will tolerate much unruliness. I imagine a big lion's paw landing on top of a mouse.

Could the U.S. Dollar Continue as the Reserve Currency?

I know that for the past 10 years, people have been talking about the U.S. dollar becoming this global reserve currency in the event of an economic meltdown, but that will never happen. This is partially because of the increased instability of the U.S. dollar. Money represents a promise by a government that that promise will be honored. The United States has already seriously jeopardized its standing in the global economy in this regard.

Also, this new currency will need to be backed with something tangible, not fiat money based on empty promises by an overextended treasury that has resorted to buying its own debt to prop up its own currency.

The U.S. dollar is also out of the running due to the fact that many nations blame the United States for much of the current economic instability.

In fact, I don't see the existing currency of any nation becoming the reserve currency. Other countries will not want to give up their own currencies and their power even symbolically by adopting an existing currency. No one nation's currency can prevail. It must be a new Coin of the Realm.

This Coin of the Realm will not declare alliance to any one nation, but to the world as a whole. It may have an inscription of some sort, maybe something like *Plures Famulus Unus, Unus Famulus Plures:* "Many Serving One, One Serving Many." This would be a pledge for the many nations to serve the one planet just as our planet serves the many people living on it.

Could the U.S. Dollar Become Worthless?

I've also heard questions about what would happen if China decided to pull the plug and let the U.S. dollar collapse. I don't think that is likely because it wouldn't be in their financial interest to allow the U.S. dollar to go to zero. Asia is a major holder of U.S. debt, which would be worth nothing if the U.S. dollar were allowed to become totally worthless.

Want to hold $50 TRILLION DOLLARS in your hand?
To get an idea how crazy hyperinflation can get, go to www
.damonvickers.com/TheDollarCrash and request your *FREE
$50 trillion dollar bill* . . . genuine, collectible legal tender from
the Reserve Bank of Zimbabwe!

What Will Happen to My Savings Denominated in U.S. Dollars?

I hear people tell me that they've got their life savings and Individual
Retirement Accounts (IRAs) invested in McDonald's, Microsoft,
Boeing, and a Vanguard index fund and they're all denominated in
U.S. dollars. They want to know what will happen. They want to
know what they can do.

First of all, you will continue to breathe. I don't believe that the
U.S. dollar will become totally worthless, but I do believe it will be
worth less. A lot less.

Now, if you have little or nothing in savings, then things won't
change much. However, if you are someone who has $20 million sit-
ting in the bank, by the time you do a workout on a currency conver-
sion, you would lose some value. You would still have the money, but
it wouldn't buy as much.

After the reset and creation of a new economic order with its new
Coin of the Realm and transaction exchange system, some kind of
orderly method of trading in the old national currencies will take place.
You will hand over your currency and get back a pile of the new currency, or a loaded debit or credit card—whatever form the new
currency takes.

This might be handled at your local branch by a bank teller with
trembling hands. Or it might be handled by some faceless, nameless
technological droid that takes your money into an ATM and spits out
something new. Or it might take place behind the closed doors of the
banks and all you'll see is a statement of your new worth. It will most
likely be some combination of all of these since it will not be a simple
process. As I said before, I don't have a crystal ball.

What Can an Investor Do to Prepare for This Crash?

We are looking at an unprecedented conflagration of events and circumstances that is totally changing the game when it comes to prioritizing how to invest your time, energy, and money. Many people have already experienced major changes in their lifestyles, and it is a given that many more people will find their world altered beyond recognition.

The fact is, there was a world before the dollar crash and there will be a world after the dollar crash. Investors who want to make it to that new world need to focus on surviving. I firmly believe that those who survive the coming rout will be able to realize a period of global economic prosperity unlike anything we have ever seen before. The purpose of this book is to help you get there.

You can own gold in some form, either tangible coins or through gold Exchange Traded Funds (ETFs). You can own silver and diamonds.

You can also explore inverse ETFs, which rise as the market falls. You'll find lists of these types of ETFs at ProShares.com and Direxion.com.

You also can own common stocks that receive a large share of their business from overseas; a falling dollar may benefit their earnings.

You can own farmland and seeds to plant for crops.

You can own certain types of rare collectibles that have proven to retain value over time. If you choose to go this route, your money won't be worth as much later, but it won't totally disappear.

I would warn people not to buy real estate like single-family homes on the market dips, because the dips will get even lower. The real estate market is simply not poised for appreciation anytime soon.

What's most important in all markets is to pay attention to the trend. Markets rise and fall, but if a market is headed down, one of the most dangerous things we can do is to try to anticipate a bottom too soon. Think of all those investors who bought Citigroup at $40 down from $50 only to see their shares fall to $0.97! In Michael Covel's book *Trend Following*, we learn that "price is all that matters."

I give the same warning about buying equities on dips. Seeming "bargains" can become bigger bargains. There is no way to tell which companies will be standing after a bear market has run its course. And even the ones still standing likely never resume being leaders when the bull market returns.

One of the First Things We Will See Is a Collapse of Bonds

I think one of the first things we will see is a collapse of bonds. This is due to a couple of things.

First, millions of investors around the world have put tons of money into bonds and into treasury securities that represent the "sovereign debt" of Westernized economies. I'm talking about the United States as well as all the Euro countries like Greece, Portugal, and France. We are talking about a huge supply of Westernized debt.

We are awash in a sea of debt, a universe full of this stuff. Right now debt is as common as sand on the beach. There is no scarcity of global debt. You'll recall that the value of anything is usually determined by supply and demand. I ask you, "Is there a shortage of global debt on the planet?" Of course not. So we have a huge supply of debt and depressed prices and few buyers. This is the first condition that leads me to talk about a pending bond apocalypse.

The second condition is that investors tend to pile into assets at the worse possible moments. They tend to go all in at the top then go all out at the bottom. To see this behavior played out, you should look at two recent market tops: the tech bubble burst in 2000 and the real estate bubble burst in 2006 and 2007.

In 2000, a heavy concentration of investors' money was in technology stocks; those prices inflated and that foretold the top. When that bubble burst, the value of those assets tumbled. In 2006 and 2007, family net worth was concentrated in real estate and prices kept rising. Since when have we seen real estate have appreciation like that? We never have. This was unprecedented.

But when does the greatest appreciation of an asset usually occur? Near market tops, that's when. That's exactly what we saw in 2006 and 2007. Real estate prices became massively inflated due to the availability of credit, and we used our increased credit to pay those inflated prices. It was totally unsustainable and we saw those assets eventually tumble.

Since 1982, and the Paul Volcker era when interest rates were roughly 21 percent to 22 percent, we have enjoyed a nice, long-term trend of rising bond prices and falling interest rates. It's been a wonderful ride, but all rides must eventually end and they usually do that when people have everything in the pool.

We know that the length and duration of every bear market is in direct proportion to the bull market that preceded it. We can see that the length and duration of this bull market in bonds has been going on now since 1982. That's more than 20 years of rising bond prices.

So here we are in 2010. With all the disruption and ups and downs of the market place over the last 10 years, we see a very, very heavy concentration of investors' wealth in bonds. This is when interest rates are not attractive! The interest rate for most of these bonds is near zero.

I have assets transferred to me all the time for management and so I get a good look at where investors' money is concentrated; many of these portfolios are coming in to us with 85 percent and 95 percent concentrations in Treasuries and municipal bonds. Given what I am seeing in the debt markets, this is very disturbing, so I get rid of those holdings quickly.

Now, if we see heavy dollar dumping, which is likely in the event of a dollar crash, we may see interest rates climb as countries compete for the available liquidity. This could create some new demand for bonds with these higher yields, and with that demand we could see a spike in bond prices. But I wouldn't recommend investors try to profit from this possibility as it would require precision timing; the markets would probably be in chaos at that point anyway, which would interfere with the execution of orders. By the time your order was executed, the profit could have come and gone. It's probably more prudent to "Just say no" to bonds right now.

Where Did All the Liquidity Go?

First, we know that on a global basis there is a shortage of basic liquidity. There is a shortage of real capital. There is no shortage of bonds. There are a lot of IOUs out there. So there is no shortage of debt, but there is a significant shortage of actual real liquidity.

Liquidity would mean that people actually pay for things. But the reason why people can't actually pay for things is that all assets have been inflated so high on a global basis, the only way people can buy things is on the installment plan. You can't buy that house for cash because a house is $3,000,000 or $5,000,000 and you don't have that kind of money in your bank account.

Secondly, on a global basis, Westernized economies around the world are scrambling to prop up their unsustainable debt load. They are trying to prop up what could become a deflation implosion. No one wants the implosion.

No one wants the price of that three-million-dollar house collapsing down to a level where real liquidity could actually buy it. That's because if we have to collapse prices for assets like stocks and real estate to where real liquidity could buy them—not credit cards, IOUs, and No Income, No Asset (NINA) loans but to where the real capital is—then we would find a lot of things trading at 90 percent to 95 percent discounts. All the people with a vested interest in the real estate game, mainly the property owners, don't want to see that happen. They are propping up the values of these assets so they won't experience pain.

We have the value of these debt instruments, these bonds, being propped up to unsupportable levels, which means they are at a market top and primed for a fall.

Here's what I believe.

I believe that with the staggering amount of debt in the world, it is going to be virtually impossible to pay it off.

The United States has $13 or $14 trillion in U.S. debt. We've got another $60 to 80 trillion in unfunded liabilities for existing social entitlements and another $40 to $50 trillion in promised new entitlements. And the United States doesn't have the money to pay for these entitlements. It doesn't exist.

What else doesn't exist is the willingness for countries to buy any more debt that would enable the United States to fund those entitlements. Therefore, the money won't be there.

And the other Westernized economies are in the same boat: more liabilities than liquidity. They won't be able to pay their debts, either.

I believe that we are moving quite potentially toward a global repudiation of debt. I think it is likely that a lot of that debt will be destroyed. It will be repudiated. It will be refused and it will be written off in negotiated workouts for perhaps even pennies on the dollar. And that's a very scary thing if you are an investor with much of your net worth invested in these so-called safe, Treasury securities.

It is my opinion that these debt instruments are some of the most worthless, dangerous investments on the planet right now. It is ironic that the investments that are sold to investors as being the safest investments on the planet are utterly not safe at all, but are worthless IOUs that should be liquidated from portfolios before the debt market collapses in an apocalyptic avalanche.

We Have Seen This Before

When the stock market peaked in 2000, I begged people to sell their Sun Microsystems, their EMCs, and their AOLs. Some people listened, but most of them didn't. Most people didn't want to hear it. At that time I had a radio show. When I called the market top in 2000, I did it on the airwaves; people were so incensed, I was thrown off the air for six months. Nobody wanted to hear the possibility that the stock market was going to go down. They threw me off the air to shut me up.

It wasn't until the NASDAQ fell 70 percent that I was offered a national talk show.

When I called the market top in 2007–2008, it was still difficult to get people to listen, to get people to sell. In truth, I called the top while the market was enjoying a last-gasp rally and nobody wanted to sell. They said, "Don't worry. I'll get out in time." I'm sure they thought so, but it didn't happen.

The truth is that the action at market tops is always too good, too thrilling, and just too tempting for participants to give it up. But unless you are willing to live with the consequences, you need to get out before it's too late. In the market it is critical to sell when you can, not when you have to.

What Happens After the Day the Dollar Crashes?

Here are some things we might see in quick response to the market upsets:

Expect shock and horror, denial, disbelief, and panic. People will panic even though they can't do anything. Expect people to stay in shock like they did in the Haitian earthquake. We won't necessarily experience the instantaneous loss of life as an earthquake, but the impact of the events will be deep and long-standing. People may become disoriented and unpredictable. It will feel like something major has changed, but we will still be breathing and eating and talking to people. Our actual living experience is not different.

Expect people to follow the money. As our current forms of exchange become ineffective, we will see bank runs as people flee to cash. It isn't that cash will be particularly valuable, but it will be an instinctive flight. It's pure panic. We will see problems with electronic money exchange systems unable to handle the rapidly changing circumstances. We will see swift changes in demand for cash, gold, and other hard assets as people attempt to grab valuable assets.

Expect quick deflation of the dollar and inflation in prices. Between the past several administrations and the Federal Reserve, we have seen a glut of fiat currency enter the market along with extreme national debt. This has caused a deliberate devaluation of the U.S. dollar. At the same time, we have too many dollars. When the U.S. dollar hits the skids and becomes significantly worth less, we will see the prices of goods shoot up. This inflation could easily exceed double- or triple-digit annual inflation and move into 7- to 10-digit hyperinflation. We've seen this occur in other circumstances when a currency became worthless, specifically Germany in the early 1920s, Hungary after World War II, Yugoslavia of the early 1990s, and most recently, Zimbabwe, where the rate of hyperinflation has been the most extreme ever seen. The United States will be the most impacted by this inflationary activity, although it will affect other currencies.

We are likely to see food lines and food riots. People need to eat, but most of them don't have their own farms. The United States is a net importer of food, so in this country most of us go to the supermarket to buy food. We are likely to see disruption in the distribution of food. Shortly after the markets shake out, we will start seeing inflation absolutely skyrocket. Regardless of what kind of currency is used, it won't buy much. We will see people selling or bartering anything that will put food on the table. We will see overcrowded food banks and soup kitchens, and in some regions we are likely to see food riots.

We can expect social norms to quickly deteriorate. Under this kind of stress, human behavior often changes for the worse. People do whatever it takes to protect what they have, to feed themselves and their families. We will very likely see an increase in crimes and mortality as well as growing transient populations in search of resources.

People dependent on entitlements may get desperate. The government will have its debt reset and may have to curb its expenses, much the same way the IMF imposed sanctions on Greece in exchange for covering 50 percent of their debt. The entitlements people have learned to depend on may come under the knife and people will need to find other kinds of resources. Suddenly cut off without funds, food, resources, and possibly without marketable skills, desperate people will seek food and shelter from those who have them. This is where having community support systems and food banks in place will help.

We may see a short-term police state. If the government and communities are prepared, which they are not, we may see some form of military order before too many people are harmed in riots. The government might also seize control of oil reserves and munitions and possibly move to confiscate guns from citizenry to prevent violent outbreaks.

We will likely see a rise in Doomsday prophets and scams. When a population is scared and vulnerable, we see opportunists ready to exploit them. Expect to see get-rich-quick schemes, offshore investment Ponzi scams, extreme fringe and political groups, Doomsday heralds, and false prophets declaring The Rapture is imminent and you can be saved for only $9.99 on a valid credit card.

Could the Next Bear Market Be Just Around the Corner?

It just might be, but not specifically because of the devaluation of the U.S. dollar. Markets certainly respond to fluctuations in currency values, along with prices of commodities like oil and gold, but stock prices have more to do with the value and earnings of companies themselves.

We must remember that the United States has already taken some severe hits due to the real estate meltdown, which wiped out about 40 percent of the value of companies across the board. Subsequently, business closures and job losses have continued to depress stock prices, and a drop in consumer spending has entrenched these losses.

Financial companies simply were gutted; other firms are down because they are unsustainable or can't compete and so we are seeing that fallout. They go out of business. They go into bankruptcy. The stock markets reflect the workings of business more than the workings of currencies. We will see a bear market because the economy is down, not specifically because the U.S. dollar has lost value.

Since March of 2009, the markets have had a rally, but this has not been a bull market. There is a distinctive difference between a rally and a bull market. A rally is a general rise in equity prices. A bull market is about economic expansion. It's about creating jobs. It's about IPOs, companies going public, and the capital markets of the world focusing their investments toward new industries and new companies and new ideas. These new companies, these new industries, these new ideas throw off jobs, and they enable investors to share in the prosperity and to have a share in the new growth that the country and the markets provide.

The main challenge facing not only the United States but all global markets and Westernized economies in particular is jobs. It is a valid concern whether the economies of the United States and Europe will be able to not only replace the jobs they have lost to Asia, but also whether they are going to have job creation in the future when new technologies and new industries arrive. Based upon the cost of production in Westernized economies like the United States, it is unlikely that is going to occur.

To prepare for a bear market, we need to watch for some telltale signs.

For the market to qualify as a bear market, two specific conditions must be present and come to a junction.

1. One of these conditions has to do with *basic price trends*. We know if the basic price trends are up, we can ride that trend, provided we've gotten in at a good price. But if we start to see erratic behavior in prices, or if we start to see repeated resistance, or we see prices start to stagnate, then we need to become even more observant for the signals that indicate the markets are beginning to roll themselves over in preparation for a downward price trend.

2. The other condition we watch for is the *element of inflated prices,* such as we've seen in recent rallies. By inflated prices I mean is the economy truly growing again or are prices rising for other reasons?

I am not looking for price increases due to self dealing. Self dealing is when this bakery sells to that pizzeria or that laundromat sells to that gas station. I'm looking for price increases due to an economy growing through job creation, through exports, through actually making things and exporting them outside of their borders and earning real capital on a global basis.

When real growth is absent, then we look to other causes for the inflated prices. Without the country functioning as a growing entity actually exporting real goods to the planet, we are more than likely to see a bear market inevitably return. I expect this next one could be the most devastating bear market that the world has ever seen as Westernized economies become aligned with global realities.

How Bad Can the Next Bear Market Get?

We only have to look to history to get an idea of how bad the next bear market can get. In the 1929 bear market, the stock market went down some 90 percent. I can tell you this: If you get a broad market decline of 90 percent, then you will see individual stocks go down more like 98 percent or 99 percent.

In 1973 and 1974, we saw the oil embargo, gas lines, tension between the Israelis and the Egyptians, and all kinds of crazy stuff in the Middle East. In that period the average stock probably sold off more than 85 percent.

During the bear market between 2000 and 2003 we saw the tech burst. We had stocks at $600 a share that were trading at $2 three years later.

And then we got the 2008 bear markets when we saw the Dow drop from 14,000 to 6,000 points. We had companies such as Citigroup falling from $50 a share to $.97 a share. Make no mistake about it. Bear markets are devastating, but at our firm, Nine Points Management and Research, we are market agnostic. We embrace bull and bear markets equally, seeking to profit from what the market gives us just as we did in both the 2000–2003 and the 2007–2008 market collapses.

Chapter 7

Shaping the New World Government Order

Governments and political leaders do not have the right to rule indefinitely. Governments rise and fall all the time. Power changes hands all the time. That is why governments work very hard to maintain the illusion of their omnipotence. In that way they maintain control and continue to grow in size, which of course, is their true goal.

We are seeing this occur around the globe right now. As governments become more cumbersome, they become more complex; I've already told you what happens to closed systems that become too complex: They experience entropy and ultimately deconstruct when they reach a certain threshold.

I believe that we are nearing that threshold in several countries. That is why I believe we will see the necessity of forming a Central Government (CG) that can operate in the New World Order.

The authority and responsibility that the CG would have would be clearly defined to protect the rights of the planet and all life.

In the following pages, I've taken the liberty of outlining some of the issues I think the CG will need to address. They are based on my beliefs of what is fair and equitable, but I also think they are reasonable even though we would certainly see a lot of resistance to their enforcement.

We Need to Limit the Growth of Governments

In the New World Order, the Central Government (CG) would need to have the power to regulate the size and growth rate of the governments of individual countries.

When a government becomes too large, it becomes a parasite on its citizenry and can significantly curtail economic growth. An overweight government can take control over the economy and the social hierarchy of a nation. It can become oppressive and use force to control its citizens.

Politicians are skilled at convincing their citizens that the government is more powerful than it actually is. But governments cannot govern people and mandate policies without the people's consensus; the only way governments can get that consensus is by convincing people that it is in their own best interest to give it.

To do this, governments use propaganda, blackmail, extortion, and distraction. They use soldiers, guns, tanks, bombs threats, and sometimes orange and yellow lights, like our Homeland Security warnings. The people go along with the government because they have been convinced that it is in their best interest to do so. Sometimes, it's the only way they can stay alive.

But in terms of sheer numbers, the citizens outnumber the people in government. When governments see their power slipping away, we can expect them to fight furiously for survival. They will up the ante on terror.

Some governments may go as far as using the same tactics used by the Nazis to intimidate, terrify, and ultimately destroy populations that attempt to unseat them from power. Some governments might not use fences, barbed wire, and machine guns, but the terror is still there. They may attempt to frighten and confuse citizens through propaganda, through misdirection, and by creating uncertainty.

But I think it is too late. People are no longer isolated and an increasing number are becoming knowledgeable about what is going on in their country and the other countries around the world.

When the numbers of people ready for a change reaches a critical mass, then entropy will progress to its ultimate and inevitable end. We will see a spontaneous deflation in the existing structures and their power bases and the beginnings of a restructuring.

Eventually we will see some sort of uprising. People could revolt. We could see civil unrest, murder, and mayhem. It might be triggered by one too many car bombings and spread like a Russian wildfire across the Middle East, or across Eastern Europe, or across South America, or across the United States of America.

I don't know how or when this will unfold. I don't know if we are looking at a five year window for individual governments to start dissolving. Or even a decade. Or even a week. It could take nine days or nine years.

I advise our leaders to take a very serious look at how they want to be remembered in the history books. Smart leaders will stop worrying about their next election. They will stop living in denial and stop wasting their time, energy, and money trying to reclaim a lifestyle and existence that will probably never return. They will stop trying to smear other candidates to make themselves look good and start working to look good due to their performance.

Smart leaders who intend to be part of the world's positive change will start going toe to toe with the huge problems facing all of us. Smart leaders will be courageous. They will show up, become visible, and let the people see them for who they are and judge them on their performance. They will take decisive action and join together to hammer out a constitution for a Central Government that can oversee the interests of this planet and the all life on it.

The new crop of leaders who align themselves with these efforts to restore order, to repair what has been damaged, and to work toward solutions to our shared global problems will be honored by future generations.

I think ultimately we will need some better method, a more equitable method to provide fair representation of the peoples of the world in the New World Order. This might be based on head count. Perhaps one representative per every 250 million people, which would put about 300 representatives into a coalition that might resemble the United Nations, but with more authority.

These people wouldn't necessarily represent a particular nation, but would represent a particular region or culture instead. This would mean that borders would be less meaningful and the need to protect those arbitrary borders would become less important.

Individual Nationalism versus Global Citizenship

I'm all for independence. That's a great thing. And I love my country and am proud of the courage and vision of our founders. So, don't think for a minute that I'm willing to give up my U.S. citizenship or give up the uniqueness that makes me American. But the United States is not the only country that has a national anthem. In fact, every country wants its citizens to have national pride. That's how they keep their identity.

This kind of indoctrination starts at a young age in most countries. Children are raised to pledge allegiance to their nation's flag. In America, several generations started their school day declaring, "I pledge allegiance to the flag of the United States of America . . . under God, indivisible . . ." and so on. Each year America celebrates the war that won our independence. We sing songs that glorify battle and praise the "rockets' red glare" that gave soldiers a glimpse of the flag they were fighting for. Other nations have similar traditions.

These traditions all go to help citizens identify with their nation and their culture and to instill in them a sense of "us" and "them." The problem with this "us and them" mindset is that this attitude of separatism creates and fuels tension, dissension, and wars. Individual nationalism is the ultimate excuse to pit one society against another. It allows people to take sides and kill each other.

This type of "us and them" thinking has been used to justify some of the most horrific human behavior our planet has ever seen. Look at the Japanese Kamikazes, the Nazi concentration camps, and the thousands of battles being fought every day somewhere in the world. And then our leaders use this attitude of individual nationalism to placate and assuage the grief of families when they see all the body bags unloaded from the military aircraft and take delivery of the remains of their own sons and daughters slaughtered in war.

But it's hard not to notice that the leaders of those governments full of national pride are not among the dead soldiers and citizens rotting in the fields and fertilizing the land. The political leaders are safe in their homes watching television and patting themselves on the back over the skillful media spin given to explain the latest casualties. It is also hard not to notice that war is hell on the environment, but downright profitable for corporations providing the materials and weapons of war.

Once we stop wasting the energy and resources used to maintain individual nationalism, once we get the self-righteous, posturing political leaders out of the way, a New World Order can get down to the business of increasing global efficiency and economic and environmental sustainability. The world's population can focus on what is truly important and stop going to war to protect the national pride of the people in power. Personally, I don't want to shoot at someone from another country. I'd much rather sit down and share a meal with him. Wouldn't you?

Maintaining National Identities within Global Citizenship

The CG should protect cultural identities . . . .

The idea of surrendering our national individualism is very threatening to most people. But I'm not talking about surrendering our national and cultural identities. I'm talking about eliminating the narrow-focused national individualism propagated by the political and corporate elite that allows them to wage and profit from war. I think any fear about eliminating individual identities and becoming some kind of giant melting pot where cultural differences are stamped out can be assuaged as long as policies are put into place and genuine effort is made to protect these distinctions.

An effective New World Order would not be about homogenizing cultures; it would be about embracing our commonality while honoring our differences. The world is full of billions of people and millions of cultural distinctions. When we see Maasai warriors doing their athletic dances, we want to preserve their traditions. The same is true with the Oktoberfest in Germany and the Japanese Cherry Blossom Festivals. These kinds of unique cultural characteristics have value and would be protected and preserved with tolerance and acceptance. We can maintain our individual distinctions and still focus on our similarities. Then we can truly start to live on this planet in harmony and embody John Lennon's dream for people to live as one.

It amazes me that the very governments that were so enthusiastic about trading with everyone else and investing with everyone else get so freaked out when their individual national identities and borders are threatened. But it's a fact, that's why I'm not saying we would be able to drop borders altogether, at least not immediately. I am saying that arbitrary national borders may no longer be as pertinent.

I think instead we might see nations represented more as states of a global government. These states or regions might be defined by some logical geographic boundary or the kinds of cultural distinctions I've already mentioned. These state-like regions might have individual flags the way individual states in the United States do.

Even if this kind of structure took shape, not everything would be managed from a single point of power. That would defeat the whole idea of fair representation. Out of necessity, some method of checks and balances would need to exist, with certain powers assumed by a CG and other responsibilities remaining with individual nations or regions. For instance, travel visas would still be needed, as well as regionalized monitoring of distribution networks and other transport. Depending on what kind of economic exchange is put in place, some kind of regional oversight might be required to manage that exchange system along with public services and law enforcement.

Let me add something here about the way politics are conducted in many countries and how I see that changing. If the New World Order government is run by representatives of segments of the global population, those representatives will need to be selected in some equitable way. They might come from a region's actual constituency or maybe they'll come from a bureau of prequalified officers. Regardless of where they originate, I would propose that they not represent some political party. Here's why.

In the United States and in other countries, political parties are used to stratify classes and create dissension within populations. This allows the party leaders to conduct endless arguments about problems instead of solving them. They get to play good cop/bad cop, but essentially, the parties are no different from each other. They all want power and control. They all court corporations for money to get that power and control. The verbiage changes but the intentions stay the same.

This kind of separatism caused by political parties would not be part of the structure of the CG. Eliminating parties would eliminate the huge cash-consuming political engines we see in our own and other countries. It would stop party cults from putting a roster of pre-paid politicians into power. It would likely streamline the process of voting everywhere, since citizens would be given the opportunity to vote strictly on issues, voting record, and character rather than being swayed by some charismatic party leader. Eliminating these polarizing parties would also incline more good leaders to come forward without fearing attacks on themselves and their families.

Protecting Cultures from Friendly Fire

The CG should protect cultural identities and also guard against unintentional harm from benevolent intentions.

What does unintentional harm from benevolent intentions mean? It means that harm is sometimes done to cultures and environments through efforts that were intended to help. This negative effect might occur because the recipient culture was unable to accommodate the change, or because of some unexpected interaction that causes harm.

I think about the good intentions of some of the largest charities in the world that seek to mitigate suffering by sending aid to Africa and South America. I think about some foundation sending aid to help starving African children. And I wonder how often this type of intervention actually compounds the problems found.

Let me give an example of what I mean. The people of Africa have lived in balance with their environment for millions of years. While droughts and warfare have contributed over the years to displacement, famine, and disease, the cultures were on their own path of evolution. With the introduction of Western ideas, these indigenous cultures have become corrupted, and now we see many Africans living in chaos and squalor, victims of violence and drug addiction: behaviors imported from our Western culture.

Think back to the western expansion in America during the 1800s. Pioneers and missionaries brought Christianity to the tribes of Indians, but they also brought diseases. Thousands of Native Americans dropped like flies from smallpox, malaria, and cholera. While history includes documentation that much of this disease was spread deliberately, the argument still stands. The damage caused by the interference of these early travelers clearly offset any of their best intentions.

More recently, we have a backlash against some efforts in humanitarian design. Young professional Gen-Y'ers in North America, Europe, and East Asia are studying design and applying their idealistic solutions overseas with the best intentions. A good example of this effort is a contraption called the Hippo Roller, which helps rural South African citizens transport more water over longer distances with less effort. It works really well but brings up complex issues.

Increasing numbers of international professionals are telling their Western counterparts to back off. For example, in India they've criticized Western-inspired projects like the One Laptop Per Child (OLPC) program saying that it's too expensive and doesn't solve the fundamental education problems in India.

In his article "Is Humanitarian Design the New Imperialism?" Bruce Nussbaum says, ". . . the Indian establishment locked OLPC out precisely because it perceived the effort as inappropriate technological colonialism that cut out those responsible for education in the country—policymakers, teachers, curriculum builders, parents. OLPC never got into China either. Or most of the large nations it had originally targeted."

According to Nussbaum, many recipients of these good deeds feel Western designers see their problems through their own eyes and not from the point of view of the locals. Others say the do-gooders are condescending and patronizing and that they have plenty of people in their countries with the talent to address their problems. So, here you have good intentions creating unwelcome results and dissention.

Replying to this article, a Pakistani said, "The efforts of Gen Y American and European do-gooders are overshadowed by actions of corporations, military, and politicians of the same nations. So on one hand the Indian man sees things like the Bhopal Disaster and the lack of accountability by Union Carbide, or Monsanto's GM seeds driving farmers to suicide, and on the other hand he sees some people trying to provide him with a cleaner water supply. To most Asians and Africans it seems like the Westerners cause destruction and at the same time some of them come bearing gifts. It's difficult to build trust in the face of such duplicity."

I'm just trying to make the point that when foreign practices or invasive organisms are introduced into a society, they can compound problems and increase suffering and discord. I believe that, like businesses in the free enterprise market, cultures should be allowed to evolve, rise, and fall along their own paths.

I'm reminded of the saying "No good deed goes unpunished." In this case, the recipients of the good deed are the ones being punished. I believe one of the responsibilities of the CG should be to ensure that even apparently benign interference in existing cultures is carefully examined for potential negative impacts on the recipients and the future generations within that culture.

Establishing Sustainable and Equitable Resource Management

The CG should have the responsibility and power necessary to place the protection and preservation of our global resources above the interests of any single entity.

We live on a planet of finite resources. At this point in time, humans have left their footprint on 75 percent of the planet. We have mined ores, cut down trees, dammed rivers, built housing tracts, and poured concrete over fertile farmland.

Not only are our resources being depleted at a fast rate, we are poisoning the earth in the process. We are bathing our land and water and our own DNA in a chemical soup of fertilizers, pesticides, hormones, and petrochemical products. We are trading health for wealth, making ourselves sicker, and adding to the costs of medical care. It's a lose-lose situation. From this point forward, we can no longer ignore the impact our blind and greedy race toward economic prosperity has on our environment.

This is a huge issue and I believe it is critical that centralized governance be put into place to eliminate the methodical, large-scale access and exploitation of natural resources for private gain at the expense of and detriment to the global environment.

I'm talking about oil drillers cutting corners to save money and killing people and damaging ecosystems. I'm talking about the damage to our aquifers by the firms drilling for natural gas. I'm talking about secret and illegal slaughter to the extinction of protected species. I'm talking about the destruction of forests and habitat for millions of animals in exchange for extremely short-term private profits. I'm talking about the fishing industry depleting our food resources in the oceans.

For example, the Environmental Defense Fund and the Seafood Watch maintained by the Monterey Bay Aquarium document the fact that the stocks of Orange Roughy off the coast of Australia have become depleted because the fishing industry didn't understand the lifecycle of that species. It turns out that fish can live 100 years and doesn't start reproducing until it is about 30 years old. Thus, when huge numbers were harvested, the fish population was depleted to a point where it will take decades to recover, and then only if fishing is prohibited.

Another dangerous aspect of this overfishing is the method used to catch the fish. Ocean bottom trawling for the fish ends up scraping the ocean bottom, which destroys habitat for hundreds of other species.

To add insult to injury, when fisheries discovered the huge schools of this fish, they hauled up everything they could and when the prices fell in a glutted market, they dumped their catch into landfills. Imagine that. One hundred years to grow a fish and we dump it in the trash. Is that not a sin before God?

With this type of decimation of our natural resources, I suspect that soon we will rely on farmed fish and farmed forests to supply the needs of the planet.

Meanwhile, the CG would likely need to form some kind of Resource Defense Force to protect natural resources and monitor corporations thoughtlessly endangering the environment. Imagine tree-huggers with guns protecting old growth forests!

I could go on, but I think I've made my point. The CG should have the responsibility and power needed to limit pollution and monitor the quality of air and water and the harvesting of mineral resources. It would monitor the way that food is produced to ensure the well-being of living beings. It would coordinate animal rights and protect wildlife and endangered species. In general, the CG should provide a larger context for the use, protection, and production of all the natural resources on this planet, be they elements or life-forms.

While this aspect of the CG would monitor the environmental balance of the planet, the free market will provide the economic balance necessary to distribute these resources.

We Can Expect a New Form of Exchange

The CG of the New World Order could be responsible for maintaining a currency or credit/debit transaction system for individuals and businesses worldwide. It might also control the creation and destruction of whatever instrument or form of currency is issued.

The United Nations just recently stated that it wants to replace the dollar as the world's reserve currency with a basket of global currencies. This indicates that the world leaders are open to some change in our currency system fairly soon. But that is not what I'm talking about when I talk about a global exchange system.

I'm talking about a single shared currency. No more exchange rates. No more bank profits from the overnight interest. No more of a lot of the methods used to profit from currency spreads. This could be called something like the Global Unification Exchange System (GUES). This could both create and administer a worldwide currency system.

This new currency could take different forms. It could be some newly minted tangible paper or metal Coin of the Realm that would replace all currencies used by all nations. It could be some secure credit/debit system accessed with finger, voice, or iris prints. It could be something completely different. I'm leaning toward a logical debit/credit system with access based on some kind of individual trait or maybe a chip in a card. Now let me leave that point and move on to the next responsibility I've identified for the CG.

The CG might set and maintain policies that govern banking, investment, and credit services to ensure proper risk management, cash reserve ratios, and full disclosure related to all kinds of trading and investing.

This book is not designed to be an exposé on monetary regulations worldwide. Even if it were, those policies are so complex and intertwined it would be a task as Herculean as cleaning the Aegean stables. But given all the commotion in the global banking and investment industry, the creation of policies to protect economic balances would be a natural extension of maintaining a global currency.

Strong regulations would need to be in place to protect the stability of the new Coin of the Realm and the CG would need to have a strict compliance policy. However, it is nearly impossible to explore what these policies might look like until an exchange system is in place. It is very possible with a new global debit/credit system that many of the current abuses will simply cease to be opportunities.

The Double-Edged Sword of Debt and Unsustainable Promises

The CG should protect nations against economic and social exploitation.

To understand what I mean by this, we just have to look at Third World countries that have been manipulated by enforced debt and exploited by the International Monetary Fund, (IMF), the World Bank, and the Inter-American Development Bank (IADB). As an example of what I'm talking about, let me refer you to the documentary *Life and Debt* by Stephanie Black. This film shows how these organizations colluded in 1977 to bring down Jamaica. It's a complicated tale, so I'll summarize it here and you can go online to see the whole story.

Jamaica is a very fertile country. The population contains remnants of a tribal culture and not so very long ago it was a fairly content and sustainable society that lived close to the land with a thriving dairy industry and a functioning agricultural economy that supplied the population with most of their needs.

Then in the 1970s the International Monetary Fund (IMF), the World Bank, and the Inter-American Development Bank (IADB) entered the picture, dangled the lure of development and Westernized prosperity in front of the country, and convinced the government to open up its market to imports. As the country racked up debt to adopt the Western lifestyle, the society lost touch with its own independent economic support systems.

In an attempt to stop the exploitation of his country, former Prime Minister Michael Manley was elected on an anti–IMF platform in 1976; in his post–independence speech he stated, "The Jamaican government will not accept anybody, anywhere in the world telling us what to do in our own country. Above all, we're not for sale." But just one year later Manley was forced to sign Jamaica's first loan agreement with the IMF due to lack of viable alternatives. This is a pattern common throughout the Third World.

At the time Black made her film, Jamaica owed more than $4.5 billion to the IMF, the IADB, the World Bank, and other agencies even though the development these loans promised has not taken place. Instead, Jamaica pays out more in interest than it makes, and the lives of the vast majority have been severely and negatively impacted. Between currency exchanges, restructured loans that increase interest payments, and wage guidelines that turn local labor into slave labor, Jamaica has seen increased unemployment, corruption, illiteracy, and violence. Food costs have soared, hospitals are dilapidated, and the disparity between rich and poor has increased dramatically and has created an ongoing economic crisis.

As part of the Free Trade Zone, Jamaica is wide open to U.S. companies wanting to relocate and exploit their deplorable economy. Yet now, due to NAFTA, even these dismal yet precious jobs are being lost to Mexico, Costa Rica, and the Dominican Republic.

The Jamaican people no longer supply their own food. They rely on imported powdered milk instead of on their once thriving dairy industry. They can't organize into unions because of the sanctions imposed by the international organizations holding all the financial cards, and they are falling into ruin. Unfortunately Jamaica is just one example of what is happening in many Third World countries that fall into debt to these all-powerful international organizations.

My point is that these international trade and monetary organizations seem to view the long-term impacts of their policies and interference through their own colored lens. Doesn't everyone want more stuff? Doesn't every country want to participate in global trade? The answer is "not necessarily."

If you give a kid a carrot, the kid eats the carrot. If you give a kid an ice-cream cone, he's going to want more ice cream. He's going to turn his nose up at the carrot, or maybe trade it for more ice cream. But he isn't going to eat the carrot if he can have ice cream instead. Look, the carrot is better for the kid and the kid would never miss the ice cream if some helpful IMF agent hadn't come into town with his cheerful little music box of an ice-cream truck and given away free samples of Rocky Road.

We must always consider the long-term impacts of interfering with any culture or economy. We must always ask if that interference will jeopardize that country's existing sustainability and well-being. We can't go around sticking our fingers into everyone else's pie just because we think it would be good for them. When we allow things to develop as they did in Jamaica, we're stealing their pie and leaving them with an empty pie tin.

An effective CG could monitor how Third World countries like Jamaica are developing and encourage the natural evolution of economic partners through free trade rather than through debt manipulation and would actively monitor such exploitation attempts.

I believe that a single common form of economic exchange, some acceptable Coin of the Realm, would eliminate much of the power that unfavorable currency arbitrage gives these money lenders. I believe the loss of this kind of leverage would lessen the likelihood of the kind of death spiral that took Jamaica down. In the best of all worlds, the CG would have a policy similar to one of America's most entrenched axioms: If it ain't broke, don't fix it.

A Centralized Governing Body Could Coordinate Emergency Response

The CG should control and coordinate response efforts to large-scale natural and man-made disasters. These could include earthquakes, tsunamis, and volcanic eruptions as well as things such as pollution issues, oil spills, and the spread of life-threatening diseases.

Right now governments are almost worthless when it comes to dealing with major disasters, either natural or man-made.

How effective was the U.S. government with Katrina? The U.S. government sat on its thumb while people evacuated to a football stadium and spent three days without water, food, or medical help; the follow-up aid has been a cruel joke.

How effective was the world in handling the 2010 Haitian earthquake? The efforts of those governments that did help was poorly coordinated and resulted in much more hardship for the Haitians than was necessary.

How about the global response to the 2010 Gulf of Mexico gusher crisis? Many countries rose up with offers of help, but in the end it was British Petroleum, the corporation with the most vested interests, who controlled all the efforts to stop the gusher and prevent further damage to the region and our shared oceans. This was like putting the fox in charge of the henhouse; our U.S. government leaders shook their heads and tossed British Petroleum the keys.

It is during crisis that governments have the opportunity to really mandate change, yet too often when faced with a crisis, leaders waffle and worry and try to be diplomatic and roll over and play dead and wait for the crisis to pass, hoping they won't have to do anything.

Why? Because they don't want to be unpopular. Look, no matter what decisions people make, someone is going to be unhappy. That does not justify government leaders rolling over and playing dead and hoping that the latest crisis will pass before they have to do anything.

How helpful were any of the world's governments in reining in the financial derivatives industry? That was a man-made disaster that should never have been permitted and wouldn't have been permitted if some centralized governing body had taken a long look at the potential for disaster and pulled a plug on the practice to begin with. It only makes sense that any investment instrument that has global impact be subject to global regulation, doesn't it?

My point is that as a global population we have passed the point where single nations can be counted on to control their greed and make choices that protect the interests of others who are impacted by those choices.

Chapter 8

Shaping the New World Social Order

The ideas for the New World Order that I've described in the preceding chapter deal mostly with governance, economics, fair use of resources, and fair treatment of nations. But there is more to the picture than those big policies. The New World Order will also affect how we as individuals live and share our lives, how we use and share resources, how we feed and care for ourselves, and how we relate to our environment.

We are in the process of evolving as a species; a major part of that evolution requires that we live more harmoniously with our environment. We need to start recognizing the interconnectedness of all living things. We need to start living *with* our resources rather than *off* our resources.

A cellular biologist named Bruce Lipton and columnist Steve Bhaerman recently wrote a book called *Spontaneous Evolution* that talks about this interconnectedness and how we are at the brink of making an incredible step forward in the growth of our species. I believe that part of that growth will include increased awareness of how we treat our world.

Let me give you an example of what I mean.

Driving to work one morning (yes, I drive to work because I live in a rural area about 40 miles from my office), I had to make a stop at the store. In the parking lot I saw a man sitting in his big 1500-horsepower truck. I watched him unwrap his plug of chewing tobacco (I told you it was rural) and throw the plastic wrapper into the parking lot.

Now, would he do that in his own backyard? Would he do that in his next door neighbor's house? He probably would not because he feels connected to his own home and to his neighbor's home. So, how then can he treat the environment so poorly?

Because it is "other." We are separated from our environment so thoroughly that we can't even comprehend that people halfway around the world breathe the same air that we breathe. It is this ability we have to separate ourselves from our environment and from all others that makes it possible for us to dishonor and exploit the environment and other people.

Herein lies the problem. We have billions of people on the planet and I would wager 99.999 percent of us act in a self-serving manner all the time. We are creating and living in our cumulative pollution and sewage. We are causing disease and toxicity and imbalances. We are creating suffering where it need not occur.

This sense of separateness must shift to a better understanding of the reality that we are all one. We all share the same biosphere. We all need water and air and food. As soon as we drew our first breath, we became connected to every other organism on earth. We can't disconnect ourselves from our biosphere and survive. Nor can we disconnect ourselves from other people and other species and survive.

We are part of the food chain and just because we have convinced ourselves that we are on the top of that food chain, it does not in fact make us better than the plankton that breeds in the coldest depths of the ocean. If we kill off other species and interrupt the current food chain, we could just as easily find ourselves somewhere in the middle of the chain as lunch for some other carnivore. And wouldn't that be fair? We're wiping out the food sources for bears and cougars, so isn't it fair that they replace those lost food sources however they can? I'm just asking. If bears and cougars could talk, they'd probably ask the same question.

My point is that we are not immune to extinction. Dinosaurs once ruled the planet and they died. Our priority must always be on keeping our biosphere healthy or we could go the way of the dinosaurs. I am talking about the survival of the human species here, nothing more and nothing less. Our future survival will depend on reducing the negative impact we have on earth.

Part of the New World Order, the shift to a sustainable world, lies in people making a shift of consciousness, a shift that acknowledges and embraces the oneness and interconnectedness of all things. The 2010 movie *Avatar* is a brilliant portrayal of the old world versus a world committed to the concept of oneness.

We are seeing this shifting consciousness in some pockets around the earth, but most individuals are still oblivious. And sometimes they have little choice. Most people on the planet are still very focused on just surviving day to day and are totally unconscious about how they harm the environment. This is especially true in Third World nations that are constantly being swept into wars; survival is a moment-to-moment experience. It is undeniably true where people just trying to feed their families are forced to clear-cut their forests and plant poppies for the drug trade.

For these people, a shift in consciousness isn't even on their radar. That means it is now the responsibility of those who have made this shift in consciousness to become very visible and very vocal and take action on the behalf of the global good. I wish we had more time for this shift in consciousness to occur everywhere, but we don't. We have run out of time. That's why I wrote this book.

I've identified a few areas where I believe we will need to see the involvement of some kind of centralized government while we are evolving into the New World Order I envision. I think we will see some sort of constitution drawn up that touches on some of these topics, so I've given it a shot here.

Where Will Our New Leaders Come From?

The CG should represent the interests of all people and all life on earth.

We will need good and fair-minded leaders who place the interests of the many above the interests of the few. These people may be elected or volunteer. There might be qualifications they must meet and their tenure might be months, years, decades, or life. I don't know how all that will look. But one thing I do know: They will be accountable for all their decisions to the people of the planet and they will be rewarded based on their results, not on expectations.

I believe we will see at least one individual come forward to lead this group. I think we will see a charismatic, singular global figure who will lead the world. That person needs to be willing to stand up and step forward. That person lives today.

Now, what I just said is a little scary. It brings up things like the Anti-Christ, but I know that people relate better to people than they do to causes. The probability is that someone is going to need to emerge and step forward and say, "I will lead. The challenges are great, but here are the solutions. I am willing to lead."

It won't be easy for someone to accept this challenge. Many people will think it is all about that person's ego or power trip. But that won't be the case. This person will come from a position of conscious unconditional love, as others before them. May we be kinder this time.

Most people don't come from this conscious level, so it will be difficult for them to understand that motive. But love is the only motive that will work. We've already seen world leaders who are driven by greed and the need for personal recognition and power. And we have seen the pain and destruction caused by those motivations.

I know people can lead from love and do great things for others. We have Mother Teresa. We have Jesus Christ. We have Buddha. We have Gandhi.

I grew up with a wonderful example of love personified in the person of Katherine Angell. You've never heard of her, but she was my great-grandmother and she was a human instrument of love unlike any I have encountered since.

Katherine Angell was extremely well connected to big, old East Coast money and she was a very powerful force in society. She could have used those resources for a lot of things including self-aggrandizement, but she didn't. She put her considerable resources to work to benefit others. She set up endowments. She spearheaded college departments. Her friends included some of the most powerful financiers in the world and Black Panther leaders making a political stance. No one was outside of her heart. She wielded power from a place of love and it worked well. So I have personal proof that it can be done.

Love is the strongest force in the universe. It is through our love for all life and our awe for all life that we can bring solutions to these problems. Our world and everything in it is a miracle. That makes us miracles, too. And if we are miracles, then we can make miracles, including turning our planet into a heaven. It is not for us to seek heaven in some abstract place. We need to create heaven here, now, on earth. And we have the power to create those miracles if we use love as our guide.

The Global Communication Evolution

The CG should ensure that communications on common electronic pathways such as the Internet be protected from interference.

The desire people have to share and push toward global connection is already a monumental trend. We are already moving toward oneness via the Internet. We are seeing this trend on Facebook, Twitter, and the endless blogs on every subject imaginable. I'm not a psychologist and I'm sure there are several sophisticated justifications for this trend, but I think I can identify a couple of main ones.

We do it because it is powerful. The Internet is still a relatively free forum. If I am talking to my friend down the street or a person living in Cyprus, what I am doing has nothing to do with government. It has everything to do with the unification of people on the planet. People are showing more of an alliance with each other who have shared interests than with the illusion of their national government.

We do it because people crave to belong. We do it because technology has had the effect of isolating people from others. We spend hours blogging about the intimate details of our lives and e-mailing strangers; I think this is an attempt to replace the intimacy of having live conversations with friends. We've lost that intimacy. Now, the world enters my home through my computer and I can have conversations with people around the world, and if I'm lucky they will be people who share my interests and can help me feel as if I belong. But I still don't know the name of my neighbor down the hall or the letter carrier who delivers my mail every day.

I think Westernized society is especially hungry for quality connection. People are recognizing on some level that regardless of how much money we have, regardless of our education, vocation, or accomplishments—or lack of any of those things—we are not happy. We are realizing that something is missing and we are looking for something meaningful in our lives. In this case, that something meaningful might just be something very old called relationships.

Other ways we might see this trend toward connecting could be an increase in shared living communities focused around common interests. We are seeing this for our aging population, but could also see it around cultural or artistic interests, or practical considerations like everyone who lives on this side of the river. I think people will begin to connect within communities that are meaningful to them.

As it becomes easier and easier to communicate with people all around the world, another barrier toward oneness is beginning to crumble. I'm talking about technology that makes it easier to communicate across languages.

Now, I don't speak Chinese, but I do speak a little Polish, a little Korean, and a few words in half a dozen other languages. This comes from my living in New York City where I encountered people from every nationality on a regular basis. In one day I might meet an East Indian, a Russian, an Israeli, an Argentinean, a Mexican, a German, and a Canadian. Not many people have the benefit of meeting so many people from so many different countries, but for me it was normal. Still, I had to figure out a way to connect; language was often a barrier and a simple smile often worked wonders.

That kind of obstacle is disappearing. Already we are seeing the use of technology to instantly translate and transcribe words between languages. This translation technology is already with us. Expect this trend to remain.

Think about that. People can connect directly with people anywhere in the world at any time. This kind of relationship-building bypasses any government or political interface or organized propaganda campaign. It's just people talking to people, finding some common ground for dialogue.

Now, the other side of all this togetherness and shared information is not so pretty. I know some people would prefer that certain kinds of information not be available on the Internet. These are things such as instructions on how to build bombs, pornography, information or images that denigrate or harm others, or criticism of government or people in leadership roles. Some cultures actively censor information about these types of subjects.

However, most Westernized societies are used to having free speech and would object to any kind of censorship. They maintain that for all the bad stuff out there, the Internet also provides a vehicle to reach and teach people. It could save lives by providing real-time surgery instructions to a doctor in Kenya, or provide instructions on how to build a fish farm to a fisherman in Japan.

Flash Mobbing—A Social Networking Phenomenon

I was watching Oprah the other day and she was talking about flash mobbing. She was talking about this event where thousands of people were dancing together and moving together in synchronous time around the world. It would be 7:00 P.M. in New York and noon in Europe and 9:00 in the morning in Japan, and 4,000 people would be dancing to the same music at the same time with the same movements.

Why are people doing that? These thousands of people dancing—they are not of the same political affiliation. No one asked if they were card-carrying Republicans, Democrats, or Communists. No one asked if someone was black, white, Chinese, Puerto Rican, or gay. No one cared; they were just dancing. What is happening here?

I think what we are seeing is a spontaneous event. Yes, it is planned, but the idea itself is spontaneous. People are synchronizing themselves with one another for a greater purpose. This is like a dress rehearsal for the big production that is taking shape on a global platform. This flash mobbing demonstrates that the barriers are gone. People are connecting to each other around the world at any time of day without words.

It is technology that is allowing this. The same technology that has isolated so many of us in our little cubicles is now connecting us, allowing us to share ideas and coordinate actions with precise timing around the world.

How do you change the hearts and minds of 4 billion people who each think differently politically, have different sexual orientations, and span generations? I think the music is a big part of it. Music goes beyond words and language. Music reaches the heart and pulls the body into action. Music is a powerful equalizer and a welcome embrace to people who have been battered by life.

Ending Our Addiction to Stimulation

Another communication trend I'm seeing has to do with our increasing addiction to stimulation. We are seeing a strong trend toward amping up reality like 3-D and high-definition (HD) television. Our brains are hooked on increasingly large doses of stimulation. It's like the person who needs coffee then graduates to Red Bull, then to one of the triple power energy drinks, and maybe even to some addictive drug like cocaine. It's like TV viewers who were happy with black-and-white images, then color, then more channels, then more intense images and more graphic content. Now viewers want the 1,080 lines of high definition and pretty soon we'll probably see upgrades to 2,400 and 3,000 lines of resolution. Hey, that's almost as real as real life!

So, I also see a trend toward amping up the human interface with technology. We all are comfortable with the click of the mouse to make magic happen in our computers. Now we have talking to computers and a natural extension of that is to have more interactivity with computers and other technology. The Wii is an example of this demand for and progression toward increased stimulation.

We Aren't as Smart as We Think We Are

It is important that at this stage of our evolution we learn to be brutally honest with ourselves because this truth is something worth fearing. Occasionally I hear someone declare with pride that "The United

States is the best-educated country in the world." Well, that might have been true once, but it isn't true anymore, so let me debunk that particular myth.

We have a nation of people who think they are educated, because government statistics have told them so. These people have views and opinions, but these views and opinions are not necessarily formulated out of their independent thought. These views and opinions are more often spoon-fed to them via national television networks, politicians, and the advertising campaigns launched by multinational corporations.

The brutal truth is that as a nation, we mouth the views and opinions that we are told to adopt. We are told how to think by the situation comedies we see on television and by the magazines that humble us with their double-spread ads of illusionary men and women. We are told what to believe by our religious leaders, our newspaper editors, and even our coworkers and bosses. We happily regurgitate these views and opinions at our PTA meetings and cocktail parties in the belief that our thoughts are important because so many people agree with us.

Yes, many Americans are educated and many have attended colleges, but we did not control the curriculum. We were taught to accept what we heard and regurgitate it back out as the truth. Look, every government incorporates a certain degree of propaganda into the educational system and the United States is no exception. But in this country, we have an advantage. We have the freedom to think for ourselves. We can find out what we weren't taught. We can question the data handed out as truth by the media.

But too many people don't choose to do that. It is much easier to simply vomit back up what other people have stuffed down our throats. So now we have hundreds of millions of supposedly educated people spouting other people's pre-packaged beliefs as if they mattered. They don't. No one's opinion matters except your own and you may have a few deep nights of the soul to finally dig through the garbage you've been fed to find out what you really believe.

Take the time to do that. Keep asking yourself what is true. When you hear yourself start repeating something you heard or read, ask yourself if that is what you truly believe or if you've just adopted someone else's opinion.

With regard to our level of formal education, I regret to say that as a society we have badly shortchanged our children. We have allowed our public school system to deteriorate to the point where the majority of children graduating and entering the workforce have few skills to help them succeed. Many can barely read or do math. They know nothing about handling their finances.

We are setting them up to fail. They leave home after 20 years of consuming chemical cocktails in their food and a 100 percent fat-filled mac 'n' cheese diet, wearing some deconstructed clothing that would pass for rags in a Third World country and nearly illiterate from 12 years in our less-than-state-of-the-art educational system, or less if they are one of the 7,000 students who drop out of high school every day in America.

We are doing the same thing to our kids that we are doing to our environment. We are trashing their future in every way possible.

These are the kids who will grow up to vote their leaders into office, who will run our businesses (or not), who will pay taxes from their minimum wage jobs, and who will be assigned the duty of caring for us in our old age. This frightens me. I don't want to be attended to in my old age by some kid who can't read, can't add, and who has to pop pills each day in order to see straight.

We have allowed our claim of being the best-educated country in the world to become hollow. But more important, we have practically guaranteed that the next generation will be incapable of regaining that status.

The Role of Religion in Our Transformation to a New World Order

The CG should be tolerant toward religious organizations and beliefs and not interfere with spiritual practices unless they exhibit violence or intolerance or interfere with the rights of other living beings.

I see religious and spiritual organizations playing a role in the actual transformation or in the governance of the planet. I see recognition of a level of consciousness that gives more credibility to the global whole than to individual self-interest. This would be more of a personal transformation as one recognizes the infinite power of love that is within us for each other.

During the transition, I do believe kindness will be important. Kindness is a powerful healer in times of stress. This might be the kindness and compassion demonstrated by Jesus or Buddha or David. It might be something as simple as the Golden Rule: Treat others as you would be treated. And that includes other species.

The reason I propose kindness as the core value of any religion is that it is so easy to do and it is so rewarding and everyone wins. It doesn't need a church or synagogue or mosque. It doesn't need a sacred text or traditional rituals. It doesn't need anything more than a smile and a helping hand.

With a truly open heart, the possibility exists for heaven to exist on earth. . . .

Connecting as One

I think people around the world are weary of being manipulated and lied to and controlled by entities that don't care about them. Yet at the same time, people are frightened of the coming changes and the New World Order that is on the horizon.

It is natural to be frightened by the unknown, but it is apathy that is the true enemy. That is why we must create communities and support systems where we can collaborate about solutions and help each other through the tough times ahead.

I believe our ultimate task is to learn to unify in Oneness and to embrace the humanity in all of us rather than perpetrating our separateness. We need to connect with others and become leaders and participants in our communities. Communities are like small governments, setting policies, collaborating for a common goal, yet small enough for individuals to be fully integrated into those policies. These can be physical communities in neighborhoods and towns, in cities, and even state-wide cooperatives. They can also be virtual communities such as we are seeing with the phenomenon of social networking.

Working together, we can turn our backs on the illusions of our lifestyles. We can reject the lies and manipulations of our leaders.

We can change our lifestyles to align with the new normal and stop depending on others to give us our values. We can use the next 7 to 10 years to create new communities and build the world we want to live in and leave to our children.

If we go back to the roots of the United States and what our country fought for, we see that we embraced differences in religion, in politics, and in opinion. By embracing these differences, we created a tolerant society that became a fertile ground for creativity.

Almost from the inception of this country, we exploded with energy and creativity. We led advancements in the sciences, in the arts, in technology. We became the envy of the world and we exported our enthusiasm and our courage. But it started with tolerance. It started with compassion. It started with the love of life itself. It started with a fierce desire of those early settlers to carve out a life that was meaningful to them. It started with sacred truths endowed by our Creator that all men are created equal and endowed with certain inalienable rights to life, liberty, and the pursuit of happiness. That is what defined our country and that is the ideology we carry in our genes.

In this day and age, I would expand those rights beyond just human beings to all living beings; to the dolphins and turtles, to the whales and eagles. That is the huge leap we must make in order to live in harmony with and on our planet. We must remember that we live in a symbiotic system where everything serves a purpose through its entire life cycle and no living creature is unimportant.

Our ecosystem is totally interdependent. If the human species is to evolve, we must be willing to accept that we do not have the right to destroy other parts of the system. And if our compassion isn't enough to convince us to live in harmony, then maybe we should remember that we are killing ourselves and our children with our carelessness.

The great thing about America is that unlike other countries, as U.S. citizens we are free to create our own future. We can create a brave new world out of the mistakes we've been making for the past several decades. We can stop thinking all the time about "what's in it for me" and start thinking about "what's in it for us."

While this book was taking shape, America celebrated Independence Day on the Fourth of July. I caught the fireworks display put on in Washington, D.C., and listened to the National Anthem as the cameras panned the crowd. I noticed that a lot of military personnel saluted while our anthem played; it occurred to me that except for those brave people in the military, most of us haven't really done anything to earn that freedom. It occurred to me that we take our freedom for granted, just as we take our air, water, and food for granted.

Many of us have been called to be brave in war, but many of us haven't. The truth is we are at war now to take back our lives and we are all being called to be brave.

Chapter 9

Consumers Will Decide How the Future Will Look

W e don't see too many buggy whips around anymore. Not too many telegraphs, either. And come to think of it, the only place I've ever seen a spittoon is at the museum. These products all have something in common. Each one is an everyday item that became obsolete when people changed how they lived their lives.

When people changed the way they traveled, communicated, and consumed tobacco, these items were no longer in demand and they, along with their related industries, were replaced by something else that the public embraced. However, these items didn't disappear overnight. Some took years, others took decades, but eventually an entire generation grew up without ever seeing any of them. That is social change.

In my investing career, I have learned to detect trends by watching the changes in social behavior. We are in a turbulent time when people are undergoing a great deal of pressure to make behavior changes and I guarantee that we will see some common everyday items become obsolete, just like the buggy whip, telegraph, and spittoon.

Consumer behavior will influence the development of new industries and the elimination of other industries. That's why I've included a list at the end of this book of some industries and companies that I believe are due for an overhaul or mothballing.

But consumer power won't just influence which businesses will thrive in the coming decades; it will influence how we live. It will cause changes in social behavior that goes beyond what we buy and sell. Consumer power can dictate how our food is produced, how our health care industry provides care, and how we care for our environment and the living creatures that share this planet with us.

This chapter focuses mostly on how changes in our consumer and social behavior will impact our health and the health of the planet. Adopt these ideas for yourself and the people around you. Consider them as points to prompt social action to advocate change. Look at them as seeds for potential businesses to meet new demand. I've said this before and I'll say it again: Changes in social behavior create social trends, and social trends prompt businesses to meet new demands for that social trend.

Consumers Will Drive the Next Big Thing

Consumers have immense power. I'm talking about the law of supply and demand. Right now we have a lot of corporations willing to help us feed our addictions for the finite resources on this planet. As long as we buy their products, their industries still thrive. If we choose to buy a different product or no product at all, then those companies will start feeling some pain. When that pain becomes great enough, they will likely choose one of the multiple choices below.

If the consumer does not buy a product, then the company that makes that product will:

- Stop making it.
- Produce a different version of that product.

- Abandon that product completely and produce something different.
- Make no changes and close shop or go bankrupt.

In our current economic environment, some companies will see the writing on the wall and start to align themselves with sustainable practices. But others will go for broke. In their resistance to change, we can expect them to play dirty and step up their efforts to grab as much short-term profit as they can.

We must do our best to prevent this kind of last-ditch grab for profit because it could accelerate already stressed ecological systems with dire results. We must watch these firms, monitoring their news releases and activity. We must make them very aware that they are being watched by their customers. We need to expose their negative activities to the public and encourage others to make choices for the greater good.

Yes, I know shutting down corporations will cost jobs. That cannot be helped. These are bigger issues. This is the future of the world's ecology we are fighting for. This is the planet where our children are going to live and hopefully be able to breed the next generation. We've enjoyed a nice fat juicy run over the past decades and now it's time for us to suck it up and make some sacrifice for the good of others and for the good of the planet. I'm sorry, but this is bigger than just you and me.

We don't have a lot of time left to make these changes. It took decades to retire the buggy whip, but we don't have decades. Our grace period is over.

Let me take you back for a little history lesson. We all know about the Crash of 1929, but not that many people understand what caused it. Just prior to the crash, society was enraptured with credit. You could buy things based on installment. People had all this credit and they had the ability to buy 10 times more than they could pay for up front. It was a wonderful thing and people got a little drunk on it.

This consumer-oriented market was a huge stimulant to company earnings and pumped up the economy. But it was hollow wealth. It was based on credit and debt. It was based on borrowing against the future. It was a giant Ponzi scheme that ended with a massive market crash. It took a very long time for real estate prices and stocks to come back.

Does this sound familiar? It should. Right now we are in the same situation. We are leveraged beyond what we can pay. We have inflated prices due to easy access to credit; we've already seen the market tumble and it could easily tumble further.

We have a small window of opportunity to catch our breath, do a reality check, and figure out what to do to correct the conditions that have brought us here.

Either we make the rational, hard choices, deal with our past excesses, and move on, or we continue printing more dollars and erode our purchasing power even further. Over the last 30 years, the U.S. dollar has dropped in value by 97 percent and we don't have a lot further we can go. That's why we need to stop right now and decide what kind of future we want to live in and leave to our children.

If you are reading this book now, you are already in a better mind-set than a lot of other people. You are already part of the shift that will transform this world into a more sustainable New World Order. You may already own gold or farmland. You may have your chicken coop and your greenhouse. You may own a gun or two. You are on your way to eliminating your debt and have curbed your consumption of fuels and goods.

But it isn't enough. You, me, and your cousin-in-law all must become proactive. We need a Renaissance, a rebirth of our entrepreneurial spirit and enthusiasm. We need to get everyone on board and making new kinds of choices every day that will move us closer to the changes we want to see in the world.

Focus on Creating Health and Alternative Treatments

We need to shift our social behavior toward more healthful living rather than focusing on all the diseases we can get. We must build a trend toward accountability for personal physical and mental health and reduce our rampant use of drugs and medical treatment that give us the illusion that they will somehow make us healthy. They don't. They just perpetuate more dependence on more drugs.

Right now we have the whole medical industry driven by technology and pills. But it wasn't so long ago that physicians used to apply leeches to extract ill humors. So, medicine can change. It is changing.

We need to create a significant change in social behavior to rectify this situation. We need to focus on reclaiming and maintaining our health rather than treating diseases after they've appeared. The more we focus on being sick, the sicker we get. That is a law of nature. You won't find it in any law book, but it governs our lives nonetheless.

We must improve and expand the use of alternative medicine and folk wisdom. Some of the smartest people I know practice alternative medicine and I know for a fact that this stuff can work a lot better than some of the Food and Drug Administration (FDA) approved stuff you can buy off the shelf. But it is hard to get these kinds of alternative treatments.

Right now it is very difficult for doctors to practice alternative medicine because the FDA has slapped restrictions on everything about what constitutes "natural." They are nitpicking over definitions, preventing proven homeopathic remedies to be made widely available, and meanwhile, they are probably pocketing the kickback money they are getting from the pharmaceutical industry's lobbyists.

Even so, we see more people explore less invasive medical care, which includes homeopathic and other alternative treatments. Colleges that teach people about these alternative treatments are opening. One happens to be Bastyr University, which originated in the Northwest. This school does a wonderful job training people in alternative treatments and natural remedies. And more and more traditional doctors are seeing the value in some of these treatments.

Reduce Dependence on Drugs

Big Pharma wants us dependent on their drugs. They don't want us healthy. They are in the marketing business, not the health care business. Open up a magazine or turn on the television and you'll see dozens of brand new miracle drugs with made up names that aren't even real words. Why? Because the products are made up solutions that will solve made up problems you didn't know you had.

I saw some statistics that about 40 percent of kids in school get some kind of medication. That should terrify you. I know it terrifies me. For example, according to MedicineNet.com, which compiles information about several health issues, between 3 percent and

5 percent of school-aged children are treated for attention deficit hyperactivity disorder to make them "manageable in the classroom," and 60 percent of those kids will end up with the disorder as adults. That translates into 4 percent of adults in the U.S. population, or 8 million adults.

Now I have some theories about why we are seeing these kinds of problems increase, but I'll get to that a little later in this chapter.

The overuse of pharmaceuticals has helped destroy our bodies' defenses. We have treated ourselves with antibiotics for everything from dangerous infections like MRSA to skinned knees and now our bodies can't fight off the superbugs that are appearing. Our bodies have become resistant to practically every antibiotic discovered by man so far and we can't defend ourselves from these new strains of disease. Just today in the newspaper I read an article about a superbug that originated in India and is starting to show up in hospitals in the United States.

Being Accountable for Our Well-Being or Opening Pandora's Box?

Only a few years ago only the rich or desperate would spend the $10,000 needed to get their genome mapped to uncover clues about any potential susceptibilities they might have for particular illnesses. Now, you can get your genome mapped for about one-tenth that cost; this has birthed a new industry. Currently, there are only a couple of companies commercially mapping genomes and as I write this book they are currently having some heated discussions with the institutions that funded their research about who has the rights to sell the results of their research. So there are already hands grabbing at this pie.

I don't know what the impact will be on society, the health care industry, and the insurance industry, but I suspect it will have some unexpected results. I don't know if it is a good thing or a bad thing. Personally, I don't think I like the idea of anyone probing into my DNA because that seems like the ultimate in privacy violation.

As long as there is demand, there will be supply, so this might evolve into an industry to pay attention to. But there are serious moral questions that will need to be addressed such as:

- Will insurance companies stop covering people with certain DNA profiles?
- In our new national health care system, will a predisposition for a disease make us a better or worse risk for a special treatment that the government gets to decide to let us have?
- Will genetic mutations be eliminated?
- Will genetic mutations and deviations be tracked?
- What about children with Down syndrome? Will people with a predisposition to having these kids be excluded from fertility treatments or other care?
- Will people with their genomes riddled with predispositions to costly diseases be charged more?
- Will supersmart people with strong constitutions and no predisposition for long-term illness get to pay less in health care premiums?
- What about the specter of potential genocide, where genome mapping is used in some way to target segments of the population?
- Most importantly, who gets to decide how this information is accessed and applied, if it is applied at all?

This is a case of our technology opening up Pandora's box: how we address these moral questions will be game changers for the human species.

Protect Our Water and Fishing Industries

Our oceans are becoming acidified by the tons of carbon dioxide that is pumped into the air and then absorbed by the oceans. The high amount of carbon dioxide in the air is changing the pH and the chemical makeup of the world's oceans. This means shellfish can no longer produce shells. It means the tiny animals at the bottom of the food chain won't be able to grow. It means the die-off of corals and fish that live off those corals. It means extinction of hundreds of ocean species. It means the normal chemical cycle of the ocean has been so altered, it will take hundreds and thousands of years for it to return to what it was just 50 years ago.

At the same time, we have corporations bent on extracting every fish they can from the ocean and overharvesting fish at all levels of the ocean. The ocean provides about 30 percent to 40 percent of the world's food. Yet oceanography scientists predict that between lost species due to the acidification of the ocean and overharvesting by the fishing industry, we could see the collapse of that food source within 40 years. In the Northwest we are already seeing oyster farms destroyed as the young oyster larvae die in the changed waters. It won't be long before we can't buy wild salmon or wild anything from the ocean.

Fishing industries must be brought under stricter control. Quotas need to be adjusted and methods of harvesting changed to protect species such as the Orange Roughy from being fished to depletion. We need to protect the food species that are able to survive in our acidified ocean, not harvest them to death.

Most of the acidification in the oceans can be traced to the increase in carbon emissions in the atmosphere from cars and factories. A whole lot of it is coming from China right now, as just this summer they passed the United States in energy consumption, which means they burned more oil, gas, and coal than the United States. That's pretty hard to do, but China is catching up and passing us fast.

Now, we don't have a lot of control over how the Chinese run their manufacturing plants, but I can tell you that they have no EPA watching anything over there and they dump chemicals and poisons in the very rivers people use for drinking water. Whole villages have epidemics of cancer and mutations and the country is running out of clean water. That's insane.

But we can do something in our own country. We can use less fossil fuel. We can drive less. We can rake leaves instead of turning on our power blowers. We can dock our water jets and park our snowmobiles. We can consume less non-renewable energy as a whole and be more conscious about what we do use.

The Health Care Industry Is Due for an Overhaul

Health care is an interesting business. I think it should be more appropriately named Sick care. We have millions of people employed in this sector and it is a huge money maker with lots of repeat customers medical workers can operate on, wire to life-support apparatus, and addict to prescription drugs until their dying day.

When you really think about it, keeping people sick could be seen as the primary business goal of the entire health care industry, because the sicker the population is, the more medical care they need and the more money into the coffin. (Excuse me. I meant *coffer*.) I can see why the government wants a piece of a health care industry with such a huge repeat customer base.

And where is the money supporting that profitable business coming from? Well, some of it comes from the consumer who got sick from drinking the poison water that gave him cancer and eating the non-nutritious food that made him overweight, and working 80 percent of his life at a stressful job that gave him a heart condition, or losing that job and having a heart attack.

Some of the money comes from taxpayers via government-administered Medicare benefits, and some of it will come from taxpayers via the government-administered Obama Care program to provide benefits to people who can't afford medical insurance.

Any way you look at it, the government and the health care industry have a vested interest in keeping Americans sick. If the government really wants people to become healthier, it would find a way to control the quality of the food we consume and really protect our water.

Overmedicating, Over-Testing, and Overcharging

I've heard for years that doctors routinely order more tests than necessary to avoid possible accusations of malpractice. I've also heard that doctors perform more surgeries than are necessary, so it appears we get more care for being sick than we do for being well. Still, we can't retire health care, no matter how inefficient and convoluted it is. So, if the industry as a whole wants to treat us like customers, then we should act like customers and demand different services. We can demand more preventative care and less intrusive practices.

Here are some areas where you can be proactive right away:

- You can keep yourself and your loved ones out of medical quicksand if you become proactive and stop believing everything the doctors say. Get second opinions for any treatment that will change the quality of life for the patient.
- Be prepared for medical appointments; have questions and do research on your condition.
- Question prescriptions and ask if there are non-drug solutions to the symptoms they want to treat; discuss homeopathic alternatives with a qualified practitioner of alternative medicine. You'll find that some medical doctors are not opposed to alternative treatments, but legally they cannot prescribe them or administer them.

A Trip to the Sick Factory

I generally feel pretty good, but about three months ago, I felt really sick. I was telling my mom about it and she was saying I must have Lyme disease or swine flu. So I went to the hospital. They didn't know what was wrong with me, so they ran some tests. They ran two tests. Nothing came up, but the bill came to about $2,000. I was there for an hour and a half and never saw a doctor. I paid the bill and they never found out what was wrong.

Now, there is something wrong with *that*. If I was running a hospital that actually wanted to cure people, I'd require a battery of tests to eliminate what *wasn't* wrong. But if I wanted future business, I'd put as many people as I could through the system with the minimum of attention, bill them, and leave them sick. That way, they would have to come back and I could charge them more money and still leave them sick.

I have to tell you that the hospital I went to was extremely fancy. It was a multimillion-dollar facility. In the Seattle area, there are dozens of these expensive hospitals. I don't know if anyone is getting healthier, but the medical industrial complex is doing quite well for itself.

These are commonsense suggestions that apply to everyone, but especially to our older generation, who require increased care.

The Basis of Geriatric Care Is Kindness

Obviously we need to address our aging population, so geriatric care would be on the list of services that need to be improved. You can do some of that by making sure that you know what kind of care you or your parent is getting. Go to their appointments with them and ask plenty of questions.

Remember that our elders were raised in an era when doctors were considered "godlike." This makes older people very reluctant to question medical authority, but you can! Be pushy. Demand attention. It could make the difference between surgery or medication, or life and death.

Also, encourage your aging parent to get exercise and engage in mental activities. Play cards and checkers with them. Make sure they get protein for their muscles and amino acids for their brains. Get them over-the-counter drugs based on herbs like Gotu Kola and Ginkgo Biloba to help their memory processes. Improve their diet and make sure they are eating more than carbohydrates, which are easy to prepare, sweet to the taste, and give an artificial energy boost that leaves them crashed out on the sofa after lunch and then unable to sleep at night. These are things you can do today.

And if you know an aging neighbor on your block, take an hour each week to check on them and share a glass of juice. Ask how they are doing and if you can run an errand for them. People in their 70s and 80s grew up in a gentler world where people took time out to check on their neighbors. In our world today, everyone is in a hurry and many of our elderly are forgotten in the rush. Your kindness would do more for their well-being than any number of pills. We are all One. Your neighbor is your parent and your child and you, yourself. Treat them with respect.

Any one of these suggestions can help improve the well-being of our elders, which can keep them off the medical rolls and out of nursing homes, allowing them the dignity of health.

Help Shape the Government's Mandated Medical Program

This is an area where we need to be very assertive. We must take a hand in structuring our new health care system in ways that support health rather than promote treatments. If you present ideas that are fiscally sound, you can create grassroots advocacy groups, stand up in town hall meetings, and generate media support for workable solutions.

I think that this health care reform has caused American citizens to table their political agendas as nothing else could. The entire medical profession should be involved in restructuring this system and not leave it to our government bureaucrats, who have repeatedly proven their lack of understanding of anything having to do with money, war, food, business, the environment, or health. Don't let them decide anything to do with your body!

This health care initiative that just passed came about due to the efforts of hundreds of lobbyists paid for by Big Pharma, insurance companies, and the medical services industry, which has a huge vested interest in how this pie is cut up and served. The day after this legislation was passed, all the drug stocks and hospital stocks went through the roof. This is what the lobbyists were working for.

As the citizens who will eventually be subjected to this new system, we need someone to back our interests. All this legislation accomplishes by expanding coverage is expand the government's taxing authority to perpetuate the current system, which is to continue to provide so-called health treatments to people who are sick.

The way this now works is a smoker with a six-pack-a-day habit and advanced emphysema is too sick to work and have medical benefits through his job, so he can throw himself on the mercy of the new health care system. The same is true with the 450-pound man who lives on supersized meals, TV dinners, and beer. Too sick to work and have private insurance, he can throw his sick, obese body on the health care system and the taxpayers will pick up the tab.

But what can the health care system do for these guys, really? Give the guy who can't breathe new lungs? No, they'll hook him up to a breathing machine and keep him alive as long as they can. Are they going to suck the fat out of the beer drinker? No, they'll feed him pills for high blood pressure, give him diet instructions he won't follow, and run interference as his systems collapse.

It's too late for these people. The taxpayer will end up paying for their bad health habits. I don't want to have my taxes raised so I can pay for health insurance for someone who is not motivated to improve his own health.

Stand Up, Make Noise, and Demand a Transparent Public Process

It is critical that citizens like you and me get involved in the coming medical reform. Pay close attention to what this national coverage pays for, who gets treatment, how those decisions to give or withhold treatment are made, and who makes them. If you have any kind of medical background, and there are millions of people who work in this area, then put your passion and understanding to work.

Anyone can stand up at a town hall. Make very loud noise in the media. You will find yourself with plenty of support if you take a stand and raise a flag others can rally around.

Our first hurdle is to make sure that those town hall meetings are held and that the public is notified in a timely manner. It is likely they will try to make all these policy decisions behind closed doors, the same way they passed the bailout bill and the health care legislation. Or schedule them on a Sunday night over a holiday weekend.

We must make sure this new health care program is hammered out in public. We need to make our political leaders accountable for this fiasco and hold them hostage in the media.

Purge Fertilizers, Pesticides, and Toxins from Our Food

From the very beginning of the process of producing food, the agriculture industry spreads poisonous pesticides and fertilizers over the land. These poisons end up in our food, in our water, and in our bodies. Right now, 65 man-made chemicals, many of which are used in pesticides, are listed as dangerous by the EPA (Environmental Protection Agency), the World Wildlife Federation, or the Centers for Disease Control.

Many of these chemicals affect our endocrine system and our brain function. The cumulative effects are cancer, Multiple Sclerosis, Parkinson's, Alzheimer's, and birth defects. The damage to the basic genetic code that we transfer from generation to generation is being compromised. Our actions are making unborn generations sick.

In addition to the damage this does to our own health and the general environment, it has practically obliterated our bee industry. I told you about the documentary on how our bees are so filled up with toxins from pesticides they can't live. They can't pollinate crops. That means no crops. Hello. Does that sound sustainable?

Consumers can have an impact here by purchasing only organically grown foods. We can blog about the big agriculture conglomerates that routinely use these toxins and create awareness that will impact the purchasing decisions of other consumers. We can write directly to those corporations protesting the use of these chemicals and letting them know you are boycotting their produce.

We can contact the companies that produce the pesticides and fertilizers and give them the same treatment, boycotting their products and letting them know why. If enough consumers create enough momentum for this kind of change, the corporations will have to respond in some way.

Purge Hormones and BPA from Our Food

I was shocked recently when I read an article in the *Seattle Times* about a long-term study on adolescent girls. The article cited a report in the journal *Pediatrics* that stated almost 25 percent of African-American girls, 15 percent of Latina girls, and more than 10 percent of Caucasian girls are reaching puberty as early as 7 years old. According to the journal, this is up significantly from an earlier report in 1997, so this trend is definitely increasing.

The journal article went on to identify factors in this change as increased body weight, decreased physical activity, and exposure to endocrine disrupters, which are chemicals that act on hormones. One of the disrupters mentioned in the report is Bisphenol A (BPA), a common additive to plastics that is also used to line the cans of many food items. Let me tell you about this stuff.

BPA is used to make polycarbonate plastic resins and epoxy resins. Polycarbonate resins are used in the manufacture of plastic food and drink containers, while epoxy resins are used to manufacture food and beverage can liners. We are talking about this stuff soaking into our canned peaches, our baby food, our baked beans, and our beer. Nearly everything that comes in a can is saturated with this stuff. And that's not the worst. This stuff is used in plastics of all kinds including water bottles, baby bottles, and toys for kids.

Humans produce more than 100 various kinds of hormones; the two major groups are estrogens and androgens (testosterone). A lot of man-made chemicals use molecular structures similar to these natural hormones, which can mimic the natural hormones and interrupt their normal functions.

Yet hormones are used in hundreds of products from acne cream to sleep preparations. They are commonly fed to livestock to promote growth. The casual use of hormones has become practically epidemic and has the potential to seriously alter the ability of living creatures to reproduce. Already wild birds, amphibians, and animals in the wild such as river otters have been studied and some populations have become sterile, changed genders, or stopped developing sexually. There is growing evidence that the human species is being affected in similar ways. This is totally insane! We must end these practices now!

Purge Sugars and Additives from Our Food

If you look at the labels of nearly all processed foods, you will find corn syrup and sugar fairly high on the list of ingredients. No wonder we have an obesity problem in this country. You will also find monosodium glutamate (MSG) listed on a lot of products, an additive that many people already avoid.

Again the consumer is in the driver's seat. When enough consumers boycott sugar-fortified foods and leave them on the shelves in favor of products without the added sweetening, we should see changes in what is put on our grocery shelves. Consumers can hurry this process by writing to the major companies that produce processed foods and ask for alternative products without the sugar and additives.

Kill Factory Farming

Factory farming is its own nightmare. It exploits workers and has one of the highest rates on worker injuries of any industry. Beyond that, many of these factories allow the raw sewage from the stockyards to flow directly into nearby rivers.

Some of these food production farms use steroids, hormones, antibiotics, and other chemicals to produce "better" meat. All those things end up in our bodies and some stay permanently. Some cause permanent changes.

Some practices in factory farming have resulted in the spread of diseases such as mad cow disease and *E. coli*. In his book *Fast Food Nation* and the film by the same name, investigative journalist Eric Schlosser talks about this industry. He also criticizes the fast-food industry and describes how McDonald's built its marketing campaign to young children on successful Walt Disney's marketing strategies. He also explains how our school systems have been infiltrated by fast-food corporations; as school funding falls, fast-food and soft drink corporations step into the breach with sponsorship money and install Coke machines in the schools' hallways and put fast food on the menu.

From a health standpoint, Americans consume too much animal protein and fats. From an economic standpoint, it costs more to raise meat than it does to raise grain. From a moral standpoint, we need to start honoring our fellow travelers on this planet. We go to supermarkets and buy packaged meats, little parts of living creatures labeled by weight and cut into bite-sized pieces. This kind of packaging enables us to detach ourselves from the suffering that is involved in the raising and barbaric slaughtering of animals for our consumption.

Refuse Genetically Altered Foods

In addition to condemning factory farming, we are looking at multinational corporations like Monsanto that exploit farmers around the world and alter our food. Just so you know, I'm putting my money where my mouth is on this company. At the time this book was being written, my company fund was short Monsanto and BP.

Monsanto enslaves nations, countries, and farmers by structuring the patents they have on the seeds they sell them. The corporation locks these communities into no-win situations where they have to pay exorbitant fees for the seeds, then have to promise any future profits to pay off debt they incurred when buying those seeds.

Meanwhile, the families are well below poverty level and are trapped in a cycle of hopeless desperation as they fall further and further into debt and eventually lose their farms. I saw a recent documentary about this situation; according to the report, the suicide rate among farmers in certain areas of India has skyrocketed. It is probably not a coincidence that these are the very areas where big seed producing corporations have a death grip on the economy.

This cycle is totally unsupportable and unsustainable. These farmers are feeding people, yet are being driven out of business, their farms put in jeopardy and their futures stolen, and it is hopeless for these farmers to get out of this trap. As far as I am concerned, the way this business does business is killing people.

Demand Changes to Fast Food

Fast foods are their own category. It is a huge industry that makes billions of dollars at the cost of our nation's health. Some chains produce some decent food, but too many are feeding their customers nothing but fat, salt, and carbohydrates and meat that is suspect.

People, I don't have to tell you that this stuff is bad for you. We all know it. Now we must do something about it. The power is with the consumer. We must boycott foods that are unhealthy for us. Put these manufacturers and users on alert and let them know they will lose their customers unless they change their practices.

A trend I'd like to see would be fast-food franchises that sell organic and healthy food and juices instead of fat, sugar, carbohydrates, chemicals, and stimulants. I've noticed McDonald's is now offering smoothies, so we might start seeing other franchises follow suit.

This is the kind of thing where social networking could make a huge difference by making this issue highly visible and calling for a national boycott day or boycott week. I wonder what the numbers for those franchises would look like after a day or a week of no sales. As consumers, we would have proven our clout.

Chapter 10

Create and Profit from the Next Big Thing

As someone who is known to have picked a number of high growth companies like Cisco, Starbucks, and Amazon that were poised to profit from significant social trends, people often ask me what I think will be the next big trend in investing. Like Starbucks was The Next Big Thing. And Cisco computer technology was The Next Big Thing. And Amazon's online book retail was The Next Big Thing.

I understand their desire to know, but it is too early to tell what kind of changes our markets will see long term. Too many changes are underway and too many possibilities are on the table right now. And most importantly, people are still undecided about how they are going to deal with the challenges we are facing.

We have some serious momentum moving us toward destruction, but humans have an amazing ability to adapt on the fly and completely reverse what had appeared to be an inevitable outcome. The Next Big

Thing will come out of how we as a society respond to our challenges, so if I had to choose a theme for The Next Big Thing, it would be sustainability.

Globally Sustainable Investing for Long-Term Profits

When I talk about successful Global Sustainable Investing (GSI), I'm talking about investing in growth trends that I judge are responsible, sustainable, and potentially profitable. Of course I want to see destructive practices end, but I also want to see sustainable practices thrive, so when I look at future trends, I look hard at how sustainable the industry is.

I look at the standard practices in that industry and the financial viability of that industry and of that company. Then, like any good investor, I look for good business models that meet the important criteria that mark a company with a high probability of success.

Of course I study the financial balance sheets of companies I'm considering, but I also look hard at their balance sheet with regard to their impact on the environment and the peoples of earth.

Think about what we do. Man has impacted 75 percent of all of the world's land. That is 75 percent of all of the terrain on the planet that is not buried by the ocean. This 75 percent has been cultivated, developed, plowed under, or suburbanized, and the majority of that activity has occurred over the last 100 years.

We need to seriously think about what kind of impact humankind will have over the next 100 years.

Socially Responsible Investing

Socially responsible investing (SRI) became popular about a decade ago as people became conscious of the kinds of discrimination and exploitation multinational corporations were exercising around the world. People cared about other people and went on record as supporting companies with good human resource practices.

These SRI instruments were usually funds that contained equities of companies that met certain profiles for treatment of their human resources, or that limited their exposure to companies that participated in certain practices such as factory farming or tobacco production. Some funds shunned companies with sweatshops in Thailand. Others screened for deforestation or other environmental abuses.

I applaud those efforts because they began creating an environment where people started to take a conscious approach to their investing. But it is important when trying to do the right thing that you don't get snookered.

Some SRI funds include companies with good track records in certain areas—say minority hiring—but those same companies might have a terrible track record when it comes to dumping pollution in the local rivers or spewing dirty smoke into the air. Or you might find a SRI fund full of companies that are responsible with regard to the environment, but exploit workers in thousands of sweatshops in Third World countries. The reason I bring this up is that you cannot assume that just because a SRI fund is socially responsible in one area, it is responsible in all areas.

As an investor, in addition to looking for companies with strong balance sheets and limited liabilities, I want that company to be in alignment with my moral values. I might not want to exploit that eight-year-old worker in the tennis shoe factory, but I do want his family to eat, so I must make a judgment call.

The Positive and Negative Sides of Social Networking and Technology

The rise in the use of technology in everyday life has both positive and negative aspects. As a social trend it is here to stay for quite a while so the industry as a whole will be supported by consumers. But I want to address some aspects of our devotion to our devices, because that devotion has a dark side.

On the positive side, technology allows us to get a lot done and to reach out around the world and connect with other people and learn about things. On the negative side, our reliance on technology can sometimes create a disconnection between people. We've lost important face time with each other. Human contact has gone by the wayside as we surf the net and leave notes for each other on our Facebook accounts.

So, technology can help people come together, but the price is a destructive disconnect between people and each other, and between people and the real world in which they live. This is what I mean.

I can sit down on a Saturday night and watch a movie of a polar bear as it travels across the tundra. And 200 years from now that video could still be around. Technology lets us experience our world through a viewfinder instead of firsthand. Yes, technology can give us virtual insight into things we might not ordinarily see, but it also separates us from real experience. We need to turn off the computer and get out and live in the real world.

Our dependence on technology to inform us about our real world frightens me. It makes us voyeurs of our planet. It disembodies the very real bodies that surround us, that make up our ecology. In some ways, our voyeurism is like watching pornography or conducting torture, both of which dehumanize the objects of our attention so we don't feel their pain. We are creating a world where our experiences are filtered and buffered by a third party, namely our computer monitor or video screen.

I think people sense this disconnection and I'm thinking that the rise in popularity of social networking must be in response to this feeling of disconnectedness caused by technology. I think that is a good thing. We need to make an effort to reconnect to the other species living on this planet and to the environment that sustains us all or we may find that technology becomes the very thing that destroys us.

Then we'll be left alone in our dark rooms with our mesmerizing monitors to watch videos of things that used to live on the planet. And that would be a tragedy of galactic proportions. Watch the movie *Soylent Green* and you'll understand what I'm talking about.

Invest in Technologies That Expand Our Sustainable Energy Sources

Already we are seeing more technologies that deliver non-fossil fuel–based energy. Many are renewable sources. We are seeing solar, wind, thermal, water and wave power, nuclear, and fission. People are exploring algae and other biofuels. Wind farms built in the 1970s are providing power to nearby cities.

There are breakthrough technologies we haven't heard of yet. For instance, I'm reading in *Investor's Business Daily* about a new device being developed in China. These devices are small energy-generating units suitable to power a home. Again, this is made in China and would be exported to the world. But I don't care. If it's better for the planet, I will demand it. My only concern is that China has such a disregard for the environment that production of this unit may do more harm than good. That would be something I have to decide based on my values and moral compass. Still, the Chinese are nothing if not pragmatic. They wouldn't be making these things if there wasn't a demand for them.

As consumers, we must make it our business to discover what alternative energy sources are available to us. We need to create a grassroots movement to research and demand that alternative energy sources be supported by government funding, given tax incentives, and reported in the media. We must create such a demand for non-fossil–based fuels that the corporations feel the kick in their backsides so hard they jump when we say jump. At the same time, we can be pushing for more affordable and more effective carbon capture technologies and insist that manufacturers adopt them.

We need to support these innovations by investing in them. For example, more wind farms are in the works, so look for opportunities in peripheral industries. That would include companies that design and install the units, the suppliers of the materials used to build them, and the delivery grids that will move the energy to the final destination.

Remember that an important part of any investment decision is doing the research. Keep your ears open to controversial issues around these alternative energy sources. For example, in California, some large wind farms are interfering with the bat migration and the bat population is suffering. In Montana, the grouse is threatened. We must understand the pros and cons of any industry or business before we invest in it.

Changes in the Auto and Transportation Industry

In terms of automobiles and transportation, people are driving smaller, lighter cars and we are starting to see graphite composites used in auto body construction. They are lightweight, incredibly strong, and the kind of stuff you could do with a design perspective is unbelievable. If this trend continues, we can look for opportunities in companies that produce these composites.

In addition to smaller, lighter automobiles, we are seeing an increase in cars that use non-petroleum energy sources. Most of the models I've seen so far are run on electricity, but electricity must still come from somewhere. I hear noise about hydrogen cells and other energy sources. Solar panels—maybe whole car surfaces could be composed of solar energy collectors. I don't know where this industry will go, but the combustion engine must be phased out.

We may see more light rail and more train usage, in which case we can look for growth in the peripheral industries that supply raw resources, produce units, and install and maintain the systems.

We may see a whole new generation of transportation vehicles that travel off the ground or underground. Who knows, maybe we'll discover anti-gravity technology and we'll see the skies filled with private hovercraft as shopping malls, or as homes, or as transport.

Weaning Ourselves Off Oil

We must end our dependence on petroleum products, and the oil industry as we now know it must sunset. From the minute drilling starts until we burn the last drop of gas in our car, oil is bad for the environment.

There are 619 rigs in the Gulf Coast. Last year we pulled out 560 million barrels of oil from the Gulf. Short term, we like having gas in our cars so we can dash to the store whenever we want. But long term, oil companies have no idea if they will be able to cap all those wells. And even supposing they do figure it out, earthquakes could pop those gushers open and we could have another Gulf disaster somewhere in the world.

Look, there is no good spin to the story of oil. There is no happy ending. Our continued use of fossil fuels pumps carbon dioxide into the air and saturates our oceans so that they become acidified and unable to sustain certain kinds of life. Long term we will see extinction of some ocean species, and what wildlife remains is constantly under the threat of being destroyed by the next oil spill.

It's like the dinosaurs are rising from the dead and coming back to rule the planet. Only it's the oil drilling corporations that are the dinosaurs.

As we seriously wean ourselves off oil, we can expect some serious resistance and repercussions from the oil companies. They will point to demand and say they're only delivering what the market wants. They will defend the jobs in the industry and all the pipeline operators and processing plants. I know it will be a big mess. Short term, they will continue drilling around the world and sending lobbyists to the governments to make sure nothing gets in their way.

The only way to sunset the oil industry is to stop using their products; the best way to accomplish that is to replace our dependence on that energy source with something that is sustainable.

The Insidious Petrochemical Industry

Petrochemicals and derivates of petroleum are their own animal. These chemicals and compounds are so insidious they have permeated practically everything you can see from floor tiles to computers to synthetic fabric, from dish soap to cosmetics to pill vials. The more of these chemicals that are released in the environment and the more synthetic compounds that are created, the more they affect the natural biochemistry that occurs in cellular reproduction and DNA.

These chemicals are not static. They constantly interact with their environment. They soak into the food they package, the air we breathe, the skin they touch. Bisphenol A or BPA has already gotten a lot of press for its destructive qualities and was banned in several states in America. It needs to be banned from the planet!

The Wonderful World of Recycling, Reusing, and Repurposing

Recycling and using recycled goods is incredibly important to the welfare of our environment. Active recycling is also about honoring your home and your environment. Westerners especially generate tons of unrecyclable garbage, but we don't notice it because we pay to have it hauled away. But imagine if you lived on one acre of land for your entire lifetime and all your garbage stayed on your land.

You would have your old cars, old tires, and dirty oil from oil changes. You'd have all your empty baked bean and beer cans, all your Styrofoam cups and packing peanuts and all your old plastic water bottles and plastic packaging. You'd have all your old appliances, garden hoses, worn out shoes, and electric toasters. Your one acre of land would be awash in trash.

Every single one of those items used labor and resources in its production. Some of those resources can be recycled, but a lot of them can't. We must learn to respect the natural resources used in all the things we discard. We must get in the habit of repairing and reusing things rather than just tossing them away. We must consciously request or arrange to use recyclable materials. Ask the fast-food restaurant to switch to recycled cardboard instead of Styrofoam.

Many of us already bring our own shopping bags to the store, but we need to be more conscious about how things are packaged, too. We must mandate that recyclable materials be used in the packaging industry.

All these decisions and actions to reuse products add up to less demand on our resources. And more importantly, they send an important message to the packagers, producers, and users of non-recyclable products. That message is that consumers are dictating demand, rather than letting corporations dictate supply. A change in our attitudes would see recycling and repurposing industries gain more ground.

Teach Your Children Well

I'm the proud father of three young girls. They do crazy things; they break a lot of things because they are kids. They broke the window shade in their bedroom, so I went to the home improvement store to buy a new window shade. I was looking around for help and saw no fewer than seven people wearing store aprons, yet no one felt motivated to help me. Finally, I had to draw their attention to me, the customer.

Because I'm sometimes motivated to give people the benefit of my wisdom, I let them know that if it weren't for people like me coming in the door to buy things, they wouldn't have a job—and that they would be a lot better off if they generated a little motivation to help me, their customer, who was putting money in their pockets. I don't know if it did any good, but sometimes I just feel compelled to get people to wake up. Sometimes I talk to people like that.

I told them about the broken window shade. They showed me their products and told me it was going to cost $45 to replace this window shade. As we discussed the situation, it became clear that the only thing holding the shade to the actual spring that pulls up the shade was glue. Well, you know what? I can buy some glue. So I bought some glue for about $3 and went home and glued the window shade back together.

Why didn't I spend the $45 and have a new window shade? Because then I would have to discard the old one and it would end up in some landfill. Because the corporations would have to cut down more trees to make the cardboard to package the new shade. Because they would have to dig more metals out of the ground to make the spring and metal parts that go on the shade. Because they would have to process more petroleum to make the glue to put it together.

I asked myself, "Which is better for the world? For my home? For my planet? For my children? Which is better?"

So I bought the glue (yes, that had to be processed somewhere from some resource), but now I have glue to repair other things that would otherwise use more resources and end up in landfills. It's a conscious decision. It cost me $3 and some time and I'm okay with that. And I showed my girls how to do their own repairs. I taught them to value and take care of what they have.

This is the type of decision that I am talking about. This requires a subtle but significant change in social behavior. This is the kind of change that will affect the balance between people and the planet. It is the kind of social change that will create a trend that will grow.

Our Costly Packaging Industry

Our packaging industry needs a serious overhaul along with the recycling industry. Why can't we have packaging made of vegetable cellulose or hemp, something that is biodegradable? Or at least recyclable.

We have cut down 97 percent of all the trees in America in the last 100 years. We've used them for building, for fuel, and to make paper and cardboards. And this was already after we'd cut down all the trees in Europe. The same thing happened in the Caribbean. Our voracious appetite for this resource is totally unsustainable, and we've nearly run out of trees.

There is a value to a forest. There is a value to a clean stream. There is a value to a clean ocean. There is a value to the sound of eagles screaming as they dive down to snag a salmon swimming upstream to spawn. And that value is infinitely greater than the short-term value of how cheap my take-out dinner is.

Right now, the economics of recycling are generally not there yet, because it is cheaper to extract new resources than recycle, but we must encourage technology to make recycling more economical, more viable, so we can stop dumping all our resources into landfills.

Stop Natural Gas Companies from Destroying Our Aquifers

I've already talked about how hydrofracking is damaging our water supply. As this book is going to press, 45 percent of all the drinking water in the United States is currently at risk from this process. And the really stupid thing is that natural gas prices have actually gone down over the last two years since these gas companies started this. It's because the natural gas from the 450,000 natural gas wells in the country is flooding an already glutted market, so of course, prices for natural gas go down and share prices for those drilling firms also go down. As I see it, there is no economic benefit to producing all this natural gas. There is only a very significant environmental cost. We are losing our aquifers for nothing!

If you want to learn more about this process, check out *Gasland* by Josh Fox, an incredible documentary about the subject.

We must demand that the practice stop immediately. We must apply extreme pressure to the neck arteries of the politicians who allowed this to happen. Write to them. Create an e-mail campaign to deluge them with your outrage. Demand they rescind access to our public lands and demand that this absolutely, irrevocably unsustainable practice be stopped.

Mothball Some of Our Drug Companies

I've talked about our overmedicated population and explained how pharmaceutical companies are in the marketing business, not the medical business. So deal with them as you would any telemarketer. Tune them out. Don't buy what they're selling. Break the habit of popping pills to fix every symptom; improve your health instead by making choices to eat better, sleep better, exercise better, and focus on being well instead of wallowing in your symptoms.

Now, I'm not saying to ignore symptoms. That's your body telling you something is out of balance and needs some attention. I'm talking about letting the drug companies tell you that you are sick, when you are simply out of balance. Don't let them dictate your condition.

Putting Your Plan into Action

I've discussed trends I'm seeing take shape and how I believe they are going to impact our society and our economy. I've given you ideas about where to put your wealth now to preserve its value and how to protect what you've already managed to accumulate. I've suggested investment strategies that could take advantage of where I believe our economy is heading.

So what do you do now? You put an investment plan into action.

Right now our dollar is not sound and conventional investment strategies based on a sound dollar will not work. What you need to focus on first is preserving the purchasing power of your dollar. Then you need to focus on generating more dollars by taking advantage of the coming changes.

To open a brokerage account with Damon Vickers & Company, either go to my web site at www.damonvickers.com or call us at 800-553-0553. If you decide to transfer an existing account to Damon Vickers & Company, the appropriate forms can be downloaded directly from my web site at www.damonvickers .com/forms. And while you're on my web site, please go to www.damonvickers.com/TheDollarCrash to download the free special report that is the companion to this book.

In Chapter 6, I told a little story about my radio career. I told how I called the market tops in 2000, and then again in 2007–2008 and how nobody wanted to hear me tell them that the markets were poised to turn. Some people listened, but most of them didn't.

It's important in these unpredictable times to understand what the market is saying day to day and not just get caught up in trading on hope. It is important to remain fluid and receptive to changes that might predict potential trends. And as I've said before, in the market it is critical to sell when you *can*, not when you have to.

My hope is that people will start paying attention to what the market is really saying and not get hurt when they misinterpret the message. My track record bears out my skill in detecting investment trends based on changes in social behavior and I've trained a team of investment consultants who specialize in my approach to investing.

We Are the Change We Want to See

In this book, I've given you ideas about ways I think we can improve our experience on this planet. I've talked about destructive industries that I've determined have allowed their greed for profits to overcome their moral obligations to the planet. What you do with the information is up to you.

Maybe you'll start an advocacy group or start an intensive letter campaign. Maybe you'll help an up-and-coming political leader take on the big dogs in these industries. Maybe you'll do nothing. That would be a shame.

But this is as close to a crystal ball as I can get. It is all conjecture because we could get hit by an asteroid next week, or North Korea could decide to take out Toledo, Ohio. Or we could see our global stock markets melt down and a new currency issued. Or avian flu could wipe out seven-eighths of the world's population. Or we could mutate into amphibians and try to live in the oceans we have turned into acid. Or maybe extraterrestrials will drop in and say, "Game Over."

In 2010, we are starting to witness the beginning of a global transformation unlike anything seen for the past thousand years, or maybe even longer. I have to believe we are at the brink of a transformation possibly as dramatic as the catastrophe that wiped out the dinosaurs so many millions of years ago. Millions of years ago. Millions. It is nearly impossible to conceive of that amount of time. It's a long, long time.

In my heart I believe that the choices we make today and the actions that we take today can move mountains and that the choices you and I make this day—this day, this very day—will determine our future. It's up to each one of us to be the change we want to see.

Have you ever watched fireflies at night and seen one light up followed by another and another until the whole night sky is blinking like a marquee on Broadway? Or birds; have you noticed how one bird changes direction and the whole flock follows? Or schools of fish? Or herds of elk? The leader sets the direction and edge runners turn the herd.

We have to be willing to become leaders and edge runners. We need to be willing to be examples, to think, plan, and act differently and show others what they can do. We need to be willing to take some risks in order to help turn the herd.

It starts with you.

It's time to turn.

About the Author

Damon Vickers is the Managing Director of Nine Points Management and Research, an investment firm located in Seattle, Washington. Vickers has called three market tops since 2000: The dot-com bust, the real estate bust, and, more recently, the financial meltdown in 2008. In that year Mr. Vickers launched a private fund that rose some 63 percent.

In the 1990s, Damon Vickers and his customers were early investors in such companies as Starbucks Coffee, Cisco Systems, and Amazon .com, to name a few. Mr. Vickers' approach can best be described as "placing capital in the path of social change," a phrase he came up with in the early 1990s in response to reporters, as a way to best describe his method of selecting investments.

A frequent guest on financial television such as the Glenn Beck Show, CNBC, Bloomberg, Fox Business, and BNN in Canada, Mr. Vickers has also been quoted on the front page of the *Wall Street Journal,* the *Washington Post,* and other established publications. Mr. Vickers has a reputation for not mincing words, occasionally causing shock and consternation among media reporters and hosts unused to his brand of candor.

It was one of these moments of candor on CNBC Asia (on October 3, 2008) that captured the attention of the financial world both internationally and across the United States. His off-the-cuff comments about the coming collapse of the U.S. dollar and the rise of a new government and New World Order appeared to catch many people off guard, even while he voiced thoughts and concerns no one else was talking about at the time.

The subsequent debt crisis in Greece and beyond, along with the continued decline of the U.S. dollar and the rise in gold prices, have given his comments credence. People are listening now.

The Day After the Dollar Crashes elaborates on Mr. Vickers' earlier comments with his views about where he believes the world is headed, and more importantly, how people can survive and thrive amid the coming changes.

Mr. Vickers lives and works in Seattle, Washington, loves the Pacific Northwest, and collects Tibetan art. He is also the managing editor of DamonVickers.com, an investment blog and resource on financial markets.

Index